Python for Data Analysis

From the Beginner to Expert
Crash Course 3.0 that will Change your
Life as a Digital Programmer Thanks to
the Minimalism of this Manual.
Deep Machine Learning and Big Data

Mik Arduino

Table of Contents

Introduction

Congratulations on purchasing *Python for Data Analysis,* and thank you for doing so.

The following chapters will discuss everything that we need to know in order to get started with the Python language and develop our skills in such a way that we are able to effectively get it to handle any data analysis project that we would like to take on. There are so many benefits that come with working on a Python data analysis project, especially for businesses who are looking for ways to beat out the competition, that it makes sense why we would want to spend some time taking a look at the steps that need to be done.

At the beginning of this guidebook, we are going to spend some time looking at the basics of coding in the Python language, and how we can make this work for our needs. We will look at the beginning information, intermediate, advanced, and intensive coding that you can do in order to learn more about this language, and see just how easy it can be to actually do some of the codes as well. When we are done, you will have a good idea of some of the codes that you are able to write, and we can use this information to help out with our own data analysis.

From there, it is time for us to dive a bit into data analysis and all of the things this entails. A data analysis can be a useful thing for many business, from those who are just starting out trying to find where they belong in the industry all the way to those who have been doing work in this industry for some time who want to learn more about their competition, their customers, and other avenues that they can take in order to really beat out the competition.

While we are on the topic, we will explore some more of the great benefits that come with data analysis as well as the steps that are necessary to make this process work for us. We can then move on to a good look at machine learning and what this process is going to entail, as well as more information about some of the libraries that you are able to use in Python that will make data analysis even more efficient than before.

There are a lot of different libraries that are able to help you out with the data analysis process, but the two main ones that are ware going to explore are Pandas and Matplotlib. Pandas is a great all-purpose kind of library that is able to help us to handle most of the steps that we want with a data analysis, and matplotlib is able to help us draw up some of the charts and figures that we need in order to really be successful and see the complex relationships that are present in our data.

There are so many benefits to learning how to work with the Python coding language, and then moving it over to provide you with some of the benefits that you need for data analysis. When you are ready to learn more about a Python data analysis, make sure to check out this guidebook to help you get started.

There are plenty of books on this subject on the market, thanks again for choosing this one! Every effort was made to ensure it is full of as much useful information as possible. Please enjoy it!

Chapter 1: Python Basics – Getting Started with Python

Welcome to the world of Python! There are a lot of things to enjoy about the Python language, and we are going to spend some of our time here looking at all of the neat things that we are able to do with this kind of coding language. We are able to work with inheritances, loops, conditional statements, namespaces, and more, before moving onto data science and machine learning. But before we are able to do that, we need to first take some time to learn the basics that come with the Python.

There are a lot of different options that we are able to work with when it is time to pick out a coding language to work with. But you will find that out of all the options that you are able to choose from, the Python coding language is going to be one of the best options out there. It is versatile, it is easy to work with, and it is going to have all of the features and the strength that you are looking for in a coding language. With this in mind, let's take a look at some of the basics that come with the Python coding language.

The Benefits of Working with Python

You will quickly find when working in this language that there are a lot of benefits of choosing the Python coding language. There may be a lot of other coding languages that you are able to go with, but they are not necessarily going to provide us with the same ease of use and the same benefits as we are able to find when it comes to working with this language. Some of the different benefits that we are able to see when it is time to start working with the Python language will include:

Python is considered a beginner language, so it is simple to work with. Many people are going to find that it is scary to get started with coding. They feel like they are going to never be able to learn how to make this happen, because they have seen these codes in the past, and worry they will never be able to get things going. However, one of the best things that happen when we are working with Python is that it is simple and easy to use.

Whether you have worked with a coding language in the past or not, you will find that the Python language is a great option. It was designed to be used by beginners and was meant to help us to see some great results in the process as well. This is great news for us because it is going to help make sure that we can get things done in our coding and will ensure that we don't get scared off before we have a chance to get started.

Python can provide us with a lot of power to handle the projects that we need. You may have read the last benefit that we talked about and been worried about how hard it would be to actually use this language for some of the things that you wanted to accomplish. But you do not have to worry. Python, while easy for a lot of beginners getting started, it still has a lot of the power that you are looking for when it is time to work with this process.

There are a lot of things that you are able to do when it is time to work with Python. It is able to handle everything that you need to work with for coding, whether it is a basic code that will help you to get started, or if it is a more complex code that is harder to handle. Python has the capabilities and the extensions that you need to handle all of the different types of coding that you would like.

There are a lot of libraries and extensions that we are able to add to the Python language. The standard library that comes with Python is going to be really strong and will provide you with a lot of the different things that you would like to do inside of machine learning and more. This is going to ensure that we see some amazing results and can help with lots of codes like we will talk about in this guidebook.

However, one of the neat things that you are going to see when it is time to work with Python is all of the additional libraries and features that we are able to handle as well. There are many libraries that are specifically meant to help out with machine learning, adding in some of the capabilities of that you need to handle science, mathematics, and more that we want to do with data analysis and machine learning.

This language is a good option to work with for data science and machine learning. There are other choices that you are able to go with when it is time to handle some of the things you would like to do with machine learning and data science, and sometimes, they may do a better job. But when you want to handle a lot of different types of processes and topics with these, then Python is able to help you get it done.

Most people are going to be happy to work with Python for all of their machine learning and data analysis needs. They know that this is an easy language to learn, which is nice if they have never done any work with coding in the past. And it still has the power and all of the additional features that are needed to ensure that the algorithms will get done each and every time that you would like. No matter what you would like to do when it comes to working with machine learning, the Python coding language will be able to handle this.

Python works well when it needs to be paired up with some of the other coding languages out there. With some of the libraries that we need to accomplish our goals of machine learning and data analysis, we will need to bring in another language in order to execute some of the things that you want out of your code. This is a great option to work with because Python is going to be able to work well with any other coding language that you would like.

There is a lot of different communities out there for Python, which can help you to get a lot of your questions and concerns answered along the way. When you run into some issues with figuring out what to do with your code, or you need some help with starting a new project, you will be able to work with this community to get the answers that you are looking for. This community can be an invaluable tool that will help you to get going no matter what your level is with coding.

As we can see here, there are a lot of different benefits that are available when you decide to work with the Python coding language. It is one of the best general-purpose languages out there for you to choose from and can help you to get a lot of the coding and other aspects of your project done in no time. Whether you just want to learn a new programming language, or you are looking to complete a data analysis or some work with machine learning, then Python is going to be the right option to help you get started.

The Basic Parts of the Python Language

Now that we have had some time to learn a bit more about the Python language and what it all entails, it is time to jump right in and learn a bit more about the Python language and what we are able to do with it. There are so many different parts that come into play, and it can be an exciting language to spend our time on as well. Knowing some of these basic parts and how they are going to work for some of your needs can make a big difference in how much you are going to be able to get out of the more complex stuff that we talk about later on in this guidebook.

The first part of our basics that we need to take a look at here is the keywords. These are going to be the parts that are reserved to tell the compiler any command that we would like. These are important because they are basically the instructions that the compiler will need to follow. You can't use them in any other place in the code, and you can't give another part of the code like a function or a variable the name of a keyword or the compiler will raise an error and not do what you want. These are important instructions to the compiler, so keep this in mind before you try to use any of them.

Next on the list is going to be the identifiers. These are going to be important to the code because there are so many of them. Despite the fact that there are a lot of choices to be made with these identifiers, you will find that they follow the same naming rules, which can make things easier for a beginner.

The first rule to remember is when you name these identifiers. You have many options when you are naming your identifiers. For example, you can rely on both uppercase and lowercase letters with naming, as well as any number and the underscore symbol. You can also combine any of these together. One thing to remember here is that you can't start the name with a number, and there shouldn't be any spaces between the words that you write out. So, you can't write out 3words as a name, but you can write out words3 or threewords. Make sure that you don't use one of the keywords that we discussed above, or you will end up with an error.

When you pick out the identifier name, you can follow the rules above, and try to pick out a name that you can remember. Later on, when writing the code, you will need to pull it back up, and if you give it a name that is difficult to remember, you could run into problems or raise errors because things aren't showing up the way that you want. Outside of these rules, you will be fine naming the identifiers anything that you want.

We can't complete a topic about the basics of Python if we don't first take a look at how to write out comments in this language. As we are writing out our codes, you may find that there are times when you need to leave an explanation or a type of note inside of the code that you are writing. This is something for you to remember or to share with other programmers but not something that needs to be run by the compiler, and it is not necessary to the code running at all. You, in fact, don't want the code to run this part of the process at all. This is where the comments are going to come in.

These comments help us to explain to others who may be looking at the code what is going on, but the compiler is going to see it and will just skip over and not mess with it at all. It will not show up in any of the programs that you write; it will only show up to those who actually take a look at the script that you wrote. The only thing that you need to do to write one of these comments is add in a # symbol ahead of the comment, and the compiler will know that it should just skip right over all of that.

As the programmer, you are able to go through and write in as many of these to your code as you would like. But it is often best to keep these just down to the minimum and the ones that make the most sense. This helps to keep the coding that you do nice and orderly and neat the whole time.

The next part of the code that we need to take a look at is the variables. These are important simply because they are going to be so common in the codes that we are writing. The variables are important because they hold onto spaces in the memory of your computer to hold onto any value that you would like. You are able to easily add in any value to the value that you would like by putting the equal sign between the two of them. It is even possible for you to take two values and add it to the same variable if you would like. These are going to be common, and as we take a look through some of the codes that we are working on throughout this guidebook, you will find that you can easily see these variables throughout.

And the final thing that we are going to take a look at in this section is the operators. These are going to be simple parts of your code, but they are still important to learn how to work with. You will find that there are a number of different types of operators that you are able to work with. You can choose to focus on the arithmetic operators, which are going to help us to write out mathematical equations in our code.

This is just one kind of operator that you are able to work with though. There are also going to be the assignment operators that will help us to assign a certain value of our choice over to a variable so that the compiler can pull them out at the right time. there can also be the comparison operators that will help us to take a look at different parts of our codes and figure out if they go with one another or not.

As we can see by going through this section, there are a lot of different basics that come with coding in the

Python language, and we only had the time to look at a few of them. In the following chapters, we are going to spend some time taking a look at a lot of the other things that we are able to do with the help of the Python language and how we will be able to use each of them. But we will take it a bit further so that you are able to start writing some of your own codes in no time.

Chapter 2: Python Intermediate Course

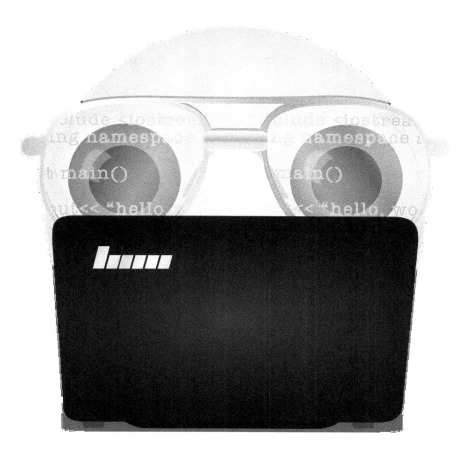

Now that we know some of the basics that come with coding in the Python language, it is time for us to move on to the next level. These types of codes that we will look at coming up next can help us to really expand what we know how to do in Python and will make it easier for us to really write the kinds of codes that we would like. In this chapter, we are going to spend our time looking at how to write loops, the importance of the classes in Python and how we can make these work, and adding in some of the decision control statements as well. Let's dive in and see what we are able to do with all of these.

Writing Your Loops

The first thing that we can take a look at when we want to move up with our skills in Python is the idea of a loop. With these loops, we are able to take a bunch of lines of our code, and squeeze it down into just a few lines instead. This makes writing codes a lot easier and also helps us to know that the codes are going to be organized and look better as well.

The loops are going to be the most useful in your code when you would like it to go through and repeat several lines many times, but you don't want to spend all of that time rewriting the code a bunch and making it look messy along the way. When you are working with some of the basics of coding, you may not think that this is really something that is necessary when you are just writing out two or three lines of code. But if you would like to have something repeat itself 100 times or more, you can see where the loop, which can take these lines and limit them to just a few, can be helpful.

For example, let's say that you want to write out a program that counted from one to one hundred for you. You could go through and handwrite the whole thing, but think about what a mess this would end up being. The loop, on the other hand, can take over on this and get all of this to show up in just a few lines of code or less to make life a little bit easier.

One thing though that we need to take into consideration when we are doing all of this is that we have to add in a condition at the end. This condition is going to be important so the code knows when to stop going through itself and when the loop is all over. If you don't add in this condition, you will just get your computer stuck and frozen, and this is never a good idea either. Having this break or a condition set up right from the beginning can help us to avoid this problem and will get the code to work the way that you want from the beginning.

With this in mind, let's take a look at some of the different types of loops that we are able to work in order to see some results and to see how this kind of process is going to work for us. The first loop on the list is the while loop. This is the best type of loop to use when you want to make sure that the code you are using is going through a cycle a certain number of times. You are able to figure out and set up how many times this is written from the beginning to ensure that the loop only goes through as often as you want.

With the while loop, your goal is not to make the code go through its cycle an indefinite amount of times, but you do want to make sure that it goes through for a specific number of times. If you are counting from one to ten, you want to make sure it goes through the loop ten times to be right. With this option, the loop is going to go through at least one time and then check to see if the conditions are met or not. So, it will put up the number one, then check its conditions and put up the number two, and so on until it sees where it is.

To give us a little bit better of an understanding on how these loops work, let's take a look at some sample codes of the while loop and see what happens:

```
counter = 1
while(counter <= 3):
        principal = int(input("Enter the principal
amount:"))
        numberofyeras = int(input("Enter the number of
years:"))
        rateofinterest = float(input("Enter the rate of
interest:"))
        simpleinterest = principal * numberofyears *
rateofinterest/100
        print("Simple interest = %.2f" %simpleinterest)
        #increase the counter by 1
        counter = counter + 1
        print("You have calculated simple interest for 3
time!")
```

While we are here, you should type in the code above to your compiler and see what will happen with it. You will see when this is executed, that the output is going to come out in a way that the user is able to place any information that they want inside of the program. Then the program will be able to do its computations and tell us what the interest rates are, based on that information, as well as the final amounts. With this example, we were able to set it up so that the loop went through three times. This is going to provide the user with a chance to try out three different items before it moves on. You can always make some changes to this though, and let it loop through more times if you wish.

With that in mind, it is time to take a look at the second type of loop, which is known as a loop. This one is often going to show up in a lot of the same situations where we find the for loop, and it is often seen as the more traditional approach to doing loops. What this means is that if you would like to keep things simple, you can usually work with the for loop and not have any problems with it at all.

To take this further, the for loop is going to be set up in a manner so that it is not the user who decides what information to give the program that will determine when it is time for the loop to stop. The loop, in this case, is going to be set up to go over the iterations in the order they are in to start the right number of times. There isn't going to be the need from an outside user or force to handle all of this, at least until the code reaches the end. An example of the code that you would be able to use to make this happen includes:

```
# Measure some strings:
words = ['apple,' 'mango,' 'banana,' 'orange']
for w in words:
print(w, len(w))
```

When you work with the for loop example that is above, you are able to add it to your compiler and see what happens when it gets executed. When you do this, the four fruits that come out on your screen will show up in the exact order that you have them written out. If you would like to have them show up in a different order, you can do that, but then you need to go back to your code and rewrite them in the right order or your chosen order. Once you have them written out in the syntax and they are ready to be executed in the code, you can't make any changes to them.

And then we can move on to the final type of loop that we are going to talk about in this guidebook. This is going to be one that is known as the nested loop. We will find that this one is unique because it is going to run a loop inside another loop to get it to work. Both of these loops will continue on their path and will keep on running until everything is done.

This is sometimes going to seem like a silly thing to add to the code, but there are a lot of times when you will write out a code, and this is needed. For example, you may find that you are working on a code where it is time to write out your own multiplication table. Maybe your goal is to write it from one to ten and have the answers lined up with this as well. This can be done with the nested loop to make things easier.

With this one, there is going to be a huge amount of code if you went through and wrote out each line of code to make this table and to get it to behave. This is something that you can do, but even as a beginner, you can see how this is going to take a lot of time and effort in order to complete. A better method to help you get this kind of thing done is to work with the following code:

#write a multiplication table from 1 to 10
For x in xrange(1, 11):
    For y in xrange(1, 11):
    *Print '%d = %d' % (x, y, x*x)*

When you got the output of this program, it is going to look similar to this:

```
1*1 = 1
1*2 = 2
1*3 = 3
1*4 = 4
```

All the way up to 1*10 = 2

Then it would move on to do the table by twos such as this:

```
2*1 =2
2*2 = 4
```

And so on until you end up with 10*10 = 100 as your final spot in the sequence.

Go ahead and put this into the compiler and see what happens. You will simply have four lines of code and end up with a whole multiplication table that shows up on your program. Think of how many lines of code you would have to write out to get this table the traditional way that you did before? This table only took a few lines to accomplish, which shows how powerful and great the nested loop can be.

The loops are great options to add to your code. There are a lot of reasons when you would need to make a loop and add it inside your code. You will be able to use it as a way to get a lot of coding done in just a few lines, and a way to clean up the code so that you can still get the same thing done without writing out too much. The compiler is set up to keep reading through the loop until the condition that you set is no longer valid. This can open up a lot of things that you are able to do with your code, while also keeping things clean and manageable all at the same time.

The Importance of Classes

One thing that is really important when it comes to working with Python is the fact that it is separated out into classes. This is going to be something that we will see a lot of when it is time to work with Python because this is the main way that we keep things organized and easy to use within the language we are writing. There are a lot of ways that we are able to describe these classes, but basically, they are going to be containers that will hold onto our objects and make sure that it is really easy to pull out the parts that we would like at the right time.

You are able to put any object that you would like into one of your classes, but we have to make sure that the object makes sense to be inside of a certain class. If you have a class that is all about fish, and you put in a plane, this is not going to make much sense. You get to choose how this works in most cases, but you have to consider what is going to work the best for your needs and think about how much sense it makes to others and to your class.

The first thing that we are going to take a look at when we focus on these classes is how to create one. To do this, we need to use the right keywords ahead of naming the class. You need to use the right keywords before naming the class. You can name this class anything that you would like, we just have to make sure that the name is right after the keyword, and that this is named something that is easier for you to remember at a later time.

After you get a chance to give your class a good name, it is time to move on to the second part, which is naming your subclass. This is the part that is going to be placed inside the parenthesis to help us stick with some of the proper rules of programming. Make sure that at the end of the first line, whenever you create a class, put in a semicolon to help you stick with some of the proper programming rules.

The good news is, that is all that we need to remember when it is time to create our own classes, and this process is often going to sound more complex than it really is. The steps that we need to use to get started with writing out some of our own classes will include:

```
class Vehicle(object):
#constructor
def_init_(self, steering, wheels, clutch, breaks, gears):
self._steering = steering
self._wheels = wheels
self._clutch = clutch
self._breaks =breaks
self._gears  = gears
#destructor
def_del_(self):
```

```
    print("This is destructor....")

#member functions or methods
def Display_Vehicle(self):
    print('Steering:' , self._steering)
    print('Wheels:,' self._wheels)
    print('Clutch:,' self._clutch)
    print('Breaks:,' self._breaks)
    print('Gears:,' self._gears)
#instantiate a vehicle option
myGenericVehicle = Vehicle('Power Steering,' 4, 'Super
Clutch,' 'Disk Breaks,' 5)


myGenericVehicle.Display_Vehicle()
```

Now, there are a lot of different things that we are able to bring up here about the code, but we are going to look at something that is likely to cross your mind at some point in all of this, and that is the process of accessing the different members of your class.

For us to get this part to work, we need to make sure that we are able to take one of the classes that we created, and then get the members of that class out. You want to make sure that the compiler and the text editor are able to recognize the classes that you have created already. This is going to help them out when it is time to execute the code in a proper manner. To do this, the code has to be set up in a proper manner. There are a few methods that we are able to use to make sure that this works for us, but we are going to work with the one known as the accessor method because this is the most common one that you will see and it is often efficient and reliable as well.

To get a better understanding of how this process works, and how you are able to access the members of your created class in a better fashion, we first need to take a look at the code below:

```
class Cat(object)
        itsAge = None
        itsWeight = None
        itsName = None
        #set accessor function use to assign values to
the fields or member vars
        def setItsAge(self, itsAge):
        self.itsAge = itsAge
```

```python
    def setItsWeight(self, itsWeight):
    self.itsWeight = itsWeight

    def setItsName(self, itsName):
    self.itsName =itsName

    #get accessor function use to return the values
from a field
    def getItsAge(self):
    return self.itsAge
    def getItsWeight(self):
    return self.itsWeight

    def getItsName(self):
    return self.itsName

objFrisky = Cat()
objFrisky.setItsAge(5)
objFrisky.setItsWeight(10)
objFrisky.setItsName("Frisky")
print("Cats Name is:," objFrisky.getItsname())
print("Its age is:," objFrisky.getItsAge())
print("Its weight is:," objFrisky.getItsName())
```

Before we move on, type this into your compiler. If you have your compiler run this, you are going to get some results that show up on the screen right away. This will include that the cat's name is Frisky (or you can change the name to something else if you want), that the age is 5 and that the weight is 10. This is the information that was put into the code, so the compiler is going to pull them up to give you the results that you want. You can take some time to add different options into the code and see how it changes over time.

The best part about these classes is that they are not really meant to be all that difficult to work with. They will make it easier for you to take care of all your information and ensure that it is in order so that things make as much sense as possible. You get the ability to create any kind of class that you would like and add in the objects that make the most sense to you, and with the way that this kind of language is set up, you know that the parts will stay in place and not move around on you at all.

How Decision Control Statements Work

The next topic that we are going to take a look at is the conditional statements. These are useful to work with when you want the computer to make some decisions on its own, no matter what kind of input you are getting from the user. It is sometimes hard to figure out what the other person is going to put into the system, and using these decision control statements or the conditional statements can make a difference in how well you are able to handle this king of thing.

When we are working with Python, there are going to be three main conditional statements that we are able to work with. These three types are going to be known as the if statement, the if else statement, and the elif statement. They will all work to help you see some great results with some of your codes, and they can be used to make sure that you reach the right solution to keep the code going, but they will do so in different ways.

Out of these three conditional statements, we are going to focus a bit on the if statement first. When we bring up the if statement, we are working with the idea of the answer from the user is either true or false. If the answer is seen as true, then we will see the progression of the code. And if it is seen as false, then we are going to see the program stop. There are already a few problems with this one we can see, but it is still an important thing to focus on for a little bit, so we are going to spend our time on it here. To give us a better idea of how these if statements work, we can take a look at the syntax below:

```
age = int(input("Enter your age:"))
if (age <=18):
        print("You are not eligible for voting, try next election!")
print("Program ends")
```

Let's explore what is going to happen with this code when you put it into your program. If the user comes to the program and puts that they are younger than 18, then there will be a message that shows up on the screen. In this case, the message is going to say "You are not eligible for voting, try next election!" Then the program, as it is, is going to end. But what will happen to this code if the user puts in some age that is 18 or above?

With the if statement, nothing will happen if the user says that their age is above 18. The if statement just has one option and will focus on whether the answer that the user provides is going to match up with the conditions that you set with your code. The user has to put in that they are under the age of 18 with the if statement in this situation, or you won't be able to get the program to happen again.

Now, we can see already where this kind of conditional statement is going to cause us some problems. Your goal here is to set it up so that the user is going to use the answer that works the best for them and their age, not the age that works best for the program. If the user is 25, you want them to put that number in without there being any problems with the system at all. This is a good example of why if the conditional statement is not going to be used all that much.

The good news is we can move on to the second kind of conditional statement and use that as a way to fix this kind of problem and still get the program to work the way that we would like. We are going to work with the if else statements now. Let's say that we are working with the same idea as before and we want to make sure that the program is going to come up with a result, no matter what input the user gives. This if else statement is going to allow us a chance to maybe have a group that is under 18, and one of the people 18 and older. The kind of code that we are able to use to make this happen includes:

```
age = int(input("Enter your age:"))
if (age <=18):
        print("You are not eligible for voting, try next election!")
else
        print("Congratulations! You are eligible to vote. Check out your local polling station to find out more information!)
print("Program ends")
```

As you can see, this really helps to add some more options to your code and will ensure that you get an answer no matter what results the user gives to you. You can also change up the message to say anything that you want, but the same idea will be used no matter the answer that the user gives.

You have the option to add in some more possibilities to this. You are not limited to just two options as we have above. If this works for your program, that is just fine to use. But if you need to use more than these two options, you can expand out this as well. For example, take the option above and expand it to have several different age groups. Maybe you want to have different options come for those who are under 18, those that are between the ages of 18 and 30, and those who are over the age of 30. You can separate it out in that way, and when the program gets the answer from the user, it will execute the part that you want.

Another example of seeing how this can work is if the program is asking one of your users to pick out which color is their favorite. You may set up the code so that there are six colors that have a message with them, such as red, purple, orange, yellow, blue, and green. It is possible that the user is going to pick out another color as their favorite, but you don't want to even try to list out all of the possible colors in the world. So, we add in the catch-all part of the else statement in order to help with this.

In this part of the code, the else statement is going to be the important part because it is going to catch all of the other answers that are possible from the user that you did not put in your code. There are obviously hundreds of colors in the world, but you don't want to go through and try to list them all out. The else statement will make sure that something still shows up on the computer, no matter what answer the user gives.

And finally, we need to take a look at the elif statements. These are a bit different than what the other two conditional statements are going to spend their time on, but you will find that they can help you to get a lot of stuff done in your codes as well, and they help make decisions too. These are going to be set up so that they give the user some choices to pick from. Depending on the answer that the user chooses, the program will make sure that the right results, which you implemented into this part of the program, will show up.

There are a lot of places where you will see these elif statements creep in. One option is in a game. If you have ever used a program or another game that gave you a menu style of choices to make, then you have seen how these elif statements work in action. These statements are a good place to start when you would like to make sure that the user has a few options to work with. You get the freedom of adding in as many of these statements into the code as you would like, we just need to ensure that the right kind of function is added into the mix as well.

The best way to learn how these elif statements are supposed to work is to actually see the syntax of one at work. A good example of this and how the elif statements are going to work will include:

if expression1:
statement(s)
elif expression2:
statement(s)
elif expression3:
statement(s)
else:
statement(s)

This is a pretty basic syntax of the elif statement, and you can add in as many of these statements as you would like. Just take that syntax and then place the right information into each part and the answer that is listed next to it. Notice that there is also an else statement at the end of this. Don't forget to add this to your code so that it can catch any answer that the user puts in that isn't listed in your elif statements.

To help you better understand how these elif statements work and how the syntax above is going to work, let's take a look at a little game that you can create using these statements:

```
Print("Let's enjoy a Pizza! Ok, let's go inside Pizzahut!")
print("Waiter, Please select Pizza of your choice from the menu")
pizzachoice = int(input("Please enter your choice of Pizza:"))
if pizzachoice == 1:
        print('I want to enjoy a pizza    apolitana')
elif pizzachoice == 2:
        print('I want to enjoy a pizza rustica')
elif pizzachoice == 3:
        print('I want to enjoy a pizza capricciosa')
else:
```

```
    print("Sorry, I do not want any of the listed
pizza's, please bring a Coca Cola for me.")
```

Now, the user is going to be able to go through and make the choices that they want, and they will get the right option to meet with them. For example, if they want to go with the pizza rustica, they will pick the number 2. If they want to have just a drink rather than one of the other choices above, they can do that too. While we did use the example of pizza in here, there are a lot of other things that you can do with it, so pretty much if you want your user to have some options, you would use the syntax that is above and then fills in the options that work the best for you.

Creating conditional statements can be a great way to make sure that your code is going to behave the way that you would like. When you are able to put all of the parts together with these conditional statements and ensure that they are set up with a response and more work that they should do when they are done with that part, then you will have a really strong program that can do some amazing things along the way.

Chapter 3: Python Advanced Course

Welcome to the Python advanced course! We have spent some time in the previous chapters looking at some of the basics that allow you to do some great stuff with Python and get some familiarity with this kind of language, and now it is time to take it to the next level. In this chapter, we are going to spend some time taking a look at some more advanced features of writing codes in Python, and options that you are going to use more as you advance your skills more and more. In this case, we are going to talk about how to write out inheritances and how to handle and raise your own exceptions. Let's take a look at how these two topics work so we can get started with them right away!

Writing Your Own Inheritances

Now that we are spending some time working on a more advanced course in Python, it is time to start out with a bit of work with the Python inheritance. These inheritances are going to be important because they allow the programmer to write out a lot of complex code, without having to go through and type this outline by line again. This will help to keep the code looking nice and organized, can save some time and will still ensure the code works the way that you would like.

To help us make sure that the inheritance is going to work the way that we would like within the code, we must remember how it works. With this, an inheritance is a process of taking the original code, which will be the base or the parent code, and then we are able to copy it down later in the code to make the derived or the child code. These derived codes are going to be adjustable, so you can add or take away parts from them, without having any negative effects on the original parent code. You are also able to choose whether to just make one derived class, or make a family tree of sorts and keep going down and reusing the code as much as you would like.

Working with an inheritance in Python is actually a lot easier to work with than it may sound in the beginning. You are able to go through this and add or take away as much information as we would like in the code to ensure that it works the way that we want. To get an idea of how to work with these inheritances, and what they are able to do for us, we can work with the following example:

```python
#Example of inheritance
#base class
class Student(object):
        def __init__(self, name, rollno):
        self.name = name
        self.rollno = rollno
#Graduate class inherits or derived from Student class
class GraduateStudent(Student):
        def __init__(self, name, rollno, graduate):
        Student__init__(self, name, rollno)
        self.graduate = graduate

def DisplayGraduateStudent(self):
        print"Student Name:," self.name)
        print("Student Rollno:," self.rollno)
        print("Study Group:," self.graduate)

#Post Graduate class inherits from Student class
class PostGraduate(Student):
        def __init__(self, name, rollno, postgrad):
        Student__init__(self, name, rollno)
        self.postgrad = postgrad

        def DisplayPostGraduateStudent(self):
        print("Student Name:," self.name)
```

```
print("Student Rollno:," self.rollno)
print("Study Group:," self.postgrad)
```

```
#instantiate from Graduate and PostGraduate classes
    objGradStudent = GraduateStudent("Mainu," 1,
"MS-Mathematics")
    objPostGradStudent = PostGraduate("Shainu," 2,
"MS-CS")
    objPostGradStudent.DisplayPostGraduateStudent
()
```

When you type this into your interpreter, you are going to get the results:

```
('Student Name:,' 'Mainu')
('Student Rollno:,' 1)
('Student Group:,' 'MSC-Mathematics')
('Student Name:,' 'Shainu')
('Student Rollno:,' 2)
('Student Group:,' 'MSC-CS')
```

Inheritances are nice because they are going to give us some freedom when it is time to write out any kind of code. If you already have a parent or a base class that you are interested in working with, and you would like to use as the basis of your derived class, this is something that we are easily able to do without having to waste time or space rewriting that code over and over again.

With this inheritance, we are able to keep some of the features that we want out of that original base class, and then we can change up the features that are not needed, or add in some new things if they will make a bit more sense for the code that we are writing. And all of this can be done to strengthen the code that we are using, without having to worry about it messing with the original code that you went through and wrote out.

You can technically go through and make as many derived classes as you want. As long as you keep doing them in order with each other and you use the example above to make your own, you can make as many of these derived classes as you would like. This makes things easier, limits the amount of code that you have to write out, and can really make things easier on you when you create a new program. Each new derived class will be able to take the features that it likes from its parent code and use them or drop them to make the code continue on and be stronger than before.

Exception Handling

The second topic that we need to take a look at in this section is about how we can not only just handle, but raise some of our own exceptions. As we are doing some work with coding in Python, you will find that there are already going to be a few exceptions that are automatically recognized by the Python language and that we are able to focus on as well. These are the ones that the library is going to see as something wrong, such as when a user is trying to divide by zero within the code that the program will raise the error message for.

However, we are also able to raise up some of our own exceptions throughout this process as well. There are some that are just for the specific program that you are writing, and you will have to tell the compiler to stop allowing it to happen. This can be used if you are creating a game or doing something else that is similar.

The first type of exception that we need to put our attention on, for now, is how to raise an exception in our own codes, and how to handle some of the automatic kinds of exceptions that the compiler will already know how to work with. We will also take a look at how to be prepared for these ahead of time, and how we can change up the error message a bit to make it more user-friendly and easy to understand.

If you are already doing some work on a code, and you notice that there is likely to be some kind of issue that will show up, or you are doing some research to figure out why something isn't working the way that you want, you will notice that there is an error or an exception, that is showing up. This happens once the compiler has a chance to look through the code and sees that there is something that isn't quite right. The good news is that usually this is a simple fix, like paying attention to what you are dividing with (you can't divide by zero in Python), or you are not spelling the name of a class or another part property.

One of the best ways to figure out how to work with these exceptions and really to see what we are doing here is to actually write it out and see it in action. A good example of one of the codes that you are able to write out in order to handle some of these exceptions will include:

```
x = 10
y = 10
result = x/y #trying to divide by zero
print(result)
```

The output that you are going to get when you try to get the interpreter to go through this code would be:

```
>>>
Traceback (most recent call last):
        File "D: \Python34\tt.py," line 3, in <module>
        result = x/y
ZeroDivisionError: division by zero
>>>
```

When you take a look at this example, your compiler is going to bring up an error, simply because you or the user is trying to divide by zero. This is not allowed with the Python code so it will raise up that error. Now, if you leave it this way and you run the program exactly how it is, you are going to get a messy error message showing up, something that your user probably won't be able to understand. It makes the code hard to understand, and no one will know what to do next.

A better idea is to look at some of the different options that you can add to your code to help prevent some of the mess from before. You want to make sure that the user understands why this exception is being raised, rather than leaving them confused in the process. A different way that you can write out this code to make sure that everyone is on the same page includes:

```
x = 10
y = 0
result = 0
try:
        result = x/y
        print(result)
except ZeroDivisionError:
        print("You are trying to divide by zero.")
```

If we type in this second code to our compiler, we will see that it is going to be similar to what we did with the first one. But it is going to take it a step further and will show us that there is a much nicer and easier to read option to read through. You will really enjoy working with this one because it helps provide your user with something that they can actually read and understand overall, rather than a message that is hard to work with.

Now, we are able to take this a bit further and look at some of the steps that you can take to raise a specialized exception. These are going to be the exceptions that you would like to see show up in your code, but are not going to be recognized automatically by the compiler of Python. Maybe you are creating a game or something else similar, and you want to be able to have that exception stop certain answers, or only allow for a certain number of guesses before it stops.

Keep in mind that when we raise our own exceptions, they are going to be unique to your code. And if you want them to show up in more than one code, you will have to raise them each time. If you do not take the time to write out these exceptions, then the compiler is not going to recognize them ahead of time at all. The neat thing is that we are able to go through and write out any kind of exception that we would like, and the idea is similar to what we were talking about before. An example of raising your own exception though will be like the following:

```
class CustomException(Exception):
def_init_(self, value):
    self.parameter = value
def_str_(self):
    return repr(self.parameter)


try:
    raise CustomException("This is a CustomError!")
except CustomException as ex:
    print("Caught:," ex.parameter)
```

When you finish this particular code, you are done successfully adding in your own exception. When someone does raise this exception, the message "Caught: This is a CustomError!" will come up on the screen. You can always change the message to show whatever you would like, but this was there as a placeholder to show what we are doing. Take a moment here to add this to the compiler and see what happens.

Handling exceptions is something that is going to show up in some of the codings we do over time and can add in another level to some of the codes that you are trying to write. As we can see here, writing out an exception that is already there and writing out one of your own customized exceptions is not that difficult a process, and you will be able to get it down and ready to go in no time at all.

Chapter 4: Python Intensive Course

In the previous chapters, we spent some time taking a look at some of the more common things that you are able to do with Python coding. The more that you learn about this language, the more complexity we are able to add to some of the codes to make them stronger. With this in mind, we have a few more intensive options that we need to look at in order to help round out some of the things that we are able to do with this language, and to ensure that we have everything we need to move onto some of the more complex aspects of this process as well. Some of the topics that we need to take a look at include:

Namespaces

When we are going through this process, we will need to work on the namespaces sometimes. For example, think back to when you were in school and you had other students in your class. How many times in those classes did you meet more than one person who had the same name as you or just the same name as each other? When this happened, when the teacher asked for a particular student, most of the time, the other students are going to ask about which one they were meaning. The teacher then would have to use some other identifying feature or another addition to the name to make sure the right student was going to answer them.

Of course, life would be easier if each person had a special name, one that no one else would share. This would help to cut out some of the confusion and you wouldn't have to go through the process to provide additional information while making sure that they were getting ahold of the right person. But since there are a limited number of names, and parents can certainly choose whatever name they would like, this is an impossible task to work with.

There is going to be an issue that is similar to working in Python and other programming languages. When a programmer is writing a short program that won't have any dependencies on outside information, it is going to be easier to provide relevant and unique names that will work with all of the different variables that you have. But, when you are working on a really long code with thousands of lines of coding, and you add in some outside modules that are all loaded up, it is going to become harder to keep with this.

➤ The good news is that we are going to see how namespaces are able to make this a bit easier. These namespaces are going to come into play when we want to give each variable and more a name that can make it unique. To understand these namespaces, we first need to look closer at why they are important, and how this namespace is going to be a system to make sure that all of the names in a program are unique. And when we can do this, it is going to help us use the variable without any conflict. With this, we are going to find that there are a few types of namespaces that are available and these include:

➤ Local namespaces: These are namespaces that are of local names inside a function. These will be created when functions are called and will only last until the functions return.

➤ Global namespaces: These namespaces will comprise of names from the different modules that you bring in to complete the project. They are created when the modules are incorporated into the project and will stick around until the script ends.

➢ Built-in namespaces: These types of namespaces consist of built-in exception names and functions.

The namespaces are going to be important when you want to write out some parts of your code. They are going to be there to help make it easier to find what is needed later on as you go through the code. They are also there to help your program learn what you would like it to pull up at a given time. If you don't take the time to give the variable, function, or another part of the code a namespace, how will your code really know what you would like to pull up at a later time when you call it up.

You also have to be careful when it is time to type in the name that you would like to give each part of the code. If your name is a bit confusing, or you are not able to remember it, then it is going to be really hard to call this up later on. If you go through and spell the name of something the wrong way, or you aren't calling it up in the proper manner, then you may find that you are going to get an error in the process. Take some caution when you create the different names of the parts of your code, and then make sure that they are names that you will be able to remember and identify later on.

There are a few rules that come with these namespaces in Python, although you still have a lot of flexibility with the name that you are using. First, you can use any character, number, and symbol that you want, such as an underscore. But you have to start with a letter. You can name something two pieces if you would like, but you can't name it 2pieces or _twopieces. If you do this, either when naming or calling up the property, you are going to end up with an error message in your program.

And one final note here is that when you create your namespaces, make sure that you don't try to give two different variables or functions the same name. This is going to cause a lot of problems in your code because the program won't know which one you want to save or call up. Give each part their own namespace so that your code can run as smoothly as possible.

Handling Strings

Now it is time for us to take a look at something that is known as the Python strings. We did take a look at these a bit with some of the other topics, but now it is time to give them a look of their own. To make this process simple, remember that this string is going to just be a series of text characters that are found in your code and can help you to get things done.

There are a few different operators that we need to focus on when we want to handle our strings in Python. An operator is going to be a simple symbol that we are able to use to perform the operations that are necessary inside of our code. Some of the operators that we need to spend the most time looking through when we work with Python include:

- Concatenation operator: This is the operator that you would want to use when it is time to concatenate strings.
- Repetition operator: This is the operator that you will use in order to create many copies of a string. You can choose how many times you would like to repeat the string.

- Slice operator: This is the operator that is going to look through your string and then retrieve the specific character that you want from there. Any time that you use this one, you would need to remember that zero is going to be the first character of the string.
- Range slice operator: This is the operator that is going to retrieve a range of characters from your index, rather than just one character. If you just want to showcase one word or one part of your string, you would use this kind of operator.
- In operator: This operator is going to search for a specified character in a target string. If the character is present somewhere in the string, then you will get an answer of True returned to you. If that character is not inside the string, then you will get an answer of False returned to you.
- No in operator: This is the operator that will work in the opposite manner as the in operator. It is going to search for a specified character in your string. But if the operator is not able to find that character in the string, then you will get the True answer returned. If that character is found in the string, then it is going to return False.

Python Functions

Functions are something that is going to show up in your code on a regular basis. These are basically a block of code that you are able to reuse in order to get a specific task done within that code. When we take the time to define a function in Python, we have to know the two main types to make sure we are using them in the proper manner. These two types are going to include user-defined and built-in functions.

The built-in functions that we are looking at are going to already come with Python, and you will just be able to use them as is. But then we have the functions that are user-defined, and these are the ones that the developer is able to create and define based on their project. However, no matter which of these functions we are working with, the functions will be treated like objects, which can make them easier to work with compared to some of the higher-level coding languages. This is going to make the functions a little bit easier to work with.

In general, a developer can either write out some of their own functions that are user-defined, or they can borrow these from a third-party library that will not be directly related back to Python. These functions are going to help us get an advantage depending on how and when we want to work with these in our code. Some of the things though that we have to remember when we are working with these functions include:

- These functions are going to be made out of code blocks that are reusable. It is necessary to only write them out once, and then you can use them as many times as you need in the code. You can even take that user-defined function and use it in some of your other applications as well.
- These functions can also be very useful. You can use them to help with anything that you want from writing out specific logic in business to working on common utilities. You can also modify them based on your own requirements to make the program work properly.
- The code is often going to be friendly for developers, easy to maintain, and well-organized all at once. This means that you are able to support the approach for modular design.
- You are able to write out these types of functions independently. And the tasks of your project can

be distributed for rapid application development if needed.

- A user-defined function that is thoughtfully and well-defined can help ease the process for the development of an application.

Now that we have a better idea about the use of Python user-defined functions, it is now time for us to take a look at a few of the arguments that you get to work with on these types of functions and then take a look at some of the coding that we are able to work with when doing this kind of function.

When it is time to work with some of these types of functions, we have to remember that it is going to take on four different types of arguments that we can work with. These are going to be types that are pre-defined, and the developer is not going to be able to change these. Instead, the developer is going to have an option to follow these rules. The four argument types that we are able to work with when it comes to these user-defined functions include:

- Default arguments: This coding language has a different way to represent the default values and the syntax for your function arguments. These default values will indicate that the function argument is going to take that value if you don't have a value for the argument pass during your function call. You will be able to tell that the default value is thereby using the equal sign (=).

- Required arguments: These are the arguments that are mandatory in your function. You need to have these values passed in the correct order and number when the function is called out, or the code isn't going to work right.

- Keyword arguments: Another option that you can work on is keyword arguments. These are also relevant to the function calls in Python. These keywords are going to be mentioned through your function call, along with some of the values that go along with this. These keywords will be mapped with the function arguments to make it easier for you to identify all the right values, even if your order doesn't stay where it should during the call. This one helps to keep everything organized in the code.

- The variable number of arguments: This is another option that you can use, and it can be useful when you don't know the exact amount of arguments that you need to pass on to a function. Or you can design it in a way where any number of arguments can be passed as long as they meet the requirements that you set.

Before we end with this, we need to take some time to write out some of these user-defined functions. Now that we have had a chance to look at the types of arguments that we are able to work with, it is time to learn the steps that you need to work with to get all of this done. There are just four basic steps that we are able to work with to make this happen and can make life a little bit easier to handle. The basic steps that we are able to work with on these functions include:

1. Declare the function you want to use. You will then need to work with the "def" keyword and then have the name of the function will come right after it.
2. Write out the arguments that you would like to use. These arguments are going to be inside the two parentheses of the function, using the arguments that we did before. End this declaration with a colon in order to help us stick

with the writing protocol that is seen as proper in this kind of language.

3. Add in the necessary statements that you would like the program to execute the proper manner.
4. End the function. You will then be able to choose whether you would like to do it with a return statement or not.

With this in mind, it is time to take a look at an example of what we are able to do with this kind of coding. An example of the kind of syntax that you are able to use to make one of these functions will include:

```
def userDefFunction (arg1, arg2, arg3, ...):
        program statement1
        program statement2
        program statement3
        ....
        Return;
```

Chapter 5: What is Data Analysis?

Now that we have been able to spend some time taking a look at the ideas of Python and what we are able to do with that coding language, it is time for us to move on to some of the things that we are able to do with all of that knowledge and all of the codes that we are looking. We are going to take a look here to see more about data analysis, and how we are able to use this to help us see some good results with our information as well.

Companies have spent a lot of time taking a look at data analysis and what it has been able to do for them. Data is all around us, and it seems like each day, tons of new information is available for us to work with on a regular basis. Whether you are a business trying to learn more about your industry and your customers, or just an individual who has a question about a certain topic, you will be able to find a wealth of information to help you get started.

Many companies have gotten into a habit of gathering up this data and learning how to make it work for their needs. They have found that there is a lot of insights and predictions inside of this data in order to make sure that it is going to help them out in the future. If the data is used in the proper manner, and we are able to gain a good handle of that data, it can be used to help our business become more successful.

Once you have gathered the data, there is going to be some work to do. Just because you are able to gather up all of that data doesn't mean that you will be able to see what patterns are inside. This is where the process of data analysis is going to come into play to help us see some results as well. This is a process that is meant to ensure that we fully understand what is inside of our data and can make it easier to use all of that raw data to make some informed and smart business decisions.

To make this a bit further, data analysis is going to be a practice where we are able to take some of the raw data that our business has been collecting, and then organize and order it to ensure that it can actually be useful. During this process, the information that is the most useful is extracted and then used from that raw data. The process of organizing and thinking about data is going to be so important here because it is the key to helping us to understand what the data does and what it doesn't contain.

There are going to be many different methods that we are able to use in order to approach this kind of data analysis, which is part of the appeal of what goes with this. We will find that with all of these methods, it is easier for us to work with a data analysis because we can make some of the adaptations that are needed to the process to ensure it works for our own needs, no matter what industry we are working in, or what our main question is in the beginning.

The one thing that we need to be careful about when we are working with data analysis, though, is to be careful about the way that we manipulate the data that we have. It is really easy for us to go through and manipulate the data in the wrong way during the analysis phase, and then end up pushing certain conclusions or agendas that are not really there. This is why we need to pay some close attention to when the data analysis is presented to us and to think really critically about the data and the conclusions that we were able to get out of it.

If you are worried about a source that is being done, and if you are not sure that you are able to complete this kind of analysis without some biases in it, then it is important to find someone else to work on it or choose a different source. There is a lot of data out there, and it can really help your business to see some results, but you have to be careful about these biases, or they will lead us to the wrong decisions in the end if we are not careful.

In addition, you will find that during the data analysis, the raw data that you will work with is able to take on a variety of forms. This can include things like observations, survey responses, and measurements, to name a few. The sources that you use for this kind of raw data will vary based on what you are hoping to get out of it, what your main question is all about, and more.

In its raw form, the data that we are gathering is going to be very useful to work with, but you may find that it is a bit overwhelming to work with as well. This is a problem that a lot of companies are going to have when they work with data analysis and something that you will have to spend some time exploring and learning more about, as well.

Over the time that you spend on data analysis and all of the steps that come with the process, the raw data is going to be ordered in a manner that makes it as useful to you as possible. For example, we may send out a survey and then will tally up the results that we get. This is going to be done because it helps us to see at a glance how many people decided to answer the survey at all, and how people were willing to respond to some of the specific questions that were on that survey.

In the process of going through and organizing the data, it is likely that a trend is going to emerge, and sometimes more than one trend. And we are going to then be able to take some time to highlight these trends, usually in the writeup that is being done on the data. This needs to be highlighted because it ensures that the person who is reading that information is going to take note.

There are a lot of places that we are going to see this. For example, in a casual kind of survey that we may try to do, you may want to figure out the preferences between men and women of what ice cream flavors they like the most. In this survey, maybe we find out that women and men are going to express a fondness for chocolate. Depending on who is using this information and what they are hoping to get out of that information, it could definitely be something that the researcher is going to find very interesting.

Modeling the data that is found out of the survey, or out of another form of data analysis, with the use of mathematics and some of the other tools out there, can sometimes exaggerate the points of interest, such as the ice cream preferences from before, in our data, which is going to make it so much easier for anyone who is looking over the data, especially the researcher, to see what is going on there.

In addition to taking a look at all of the data that you have collected and sorted through, you will need to do a few other parts as well. These are all meant to help the person who needs this information to read through it and really see what is inside and what they are able to do with all of that data. It is the way that they are able to use the information in order to really see what is going on, the complex relationships that are there, and so much more.

This means that we need to spend our time with some writeups of the data, graphs, charts, and other ways to represent and show the data to those who need it the most. This will form one of the final steps that come with data analysis. These methods are designed in a manner to distill and refine the data so that the readers are then able to glean some of the interesting information from it, without having to actually go back through the raw data and figure out what is there all on their own.

Summarizing the data in these steps is going to be critical, and it needs to be done in a good and steady manner as well. Doing this is going to be critical to helping to support some of the arguments that are made with that data, as is presenting the data in a clear and understandable manner. During this phase, we have to remember that it is not always possible that the person who needs that summary and who will use it to make some important decisions for the business will be data scientists, and they need it all written out in a simple and easy to understand this information. This is why the data has to be written out in a manner that is easy to understand and read through.

Often this is going to be done with some sort of data visualization. There are many choices of visuals that we are able to work with, and working with some kind of graph or chart is a good option as well. Working with the method that is the best for your needs and the data that we are working with is going to be the best way to determine the visual that is going to be the best for you.

Many times, reading through information that is in a more graphical format is going to be easier to work with than just reading through the data and hoping it to work the best way possible. You could just have it all in a written form if you would like, but this is not going to be as easy to read through nor as efficient. To see some of those complex relationships quickly and efficiently, working with a visual is going to be one of the best options to choose from.

Even though we need to spend some time working with a visual of the data to make it easier to work with and understand, it is fine to add in some of the raw data as the appendix, rather than just throwing it out. This allows the person who is going to work with that data on a regular basis a chance to check your resources and your specific numbers and can really help to bolster some of the results that you are getting overall.

If you are the one who is getting the results of the data analysis, make sure that when you get the conclusions and the summarized data from your data scientist that you go through and view them in a more critical manner. You should take the time to ask where the data comes from is going to be important, and you should also take some time to ask about the method of sampling that was used for all of this as well when the data was collected. Knowing the size of the sample is important as well.

This is going to allow you a chance to really learn more about the data that you have in front of you and then will allow you a chance to figure out if you can actually use the data, or if there may be some kind of bias that comes with it along the way. If the source of the data, or at least one of the sources, seems to have some kind of conflict that you are worried about, then this is going to pull your results into question, and you at least need to look it over.

Likewise, if you have some data that is gathered up from just a small sample or a sample that you worry is not really random, then it is maybe not the best data to work with. The good news is that researchers who are reputable are going to have no problem providing you with the information that you need about the techniques of data gathering that they used and more so that you can make some important decisions about whether this data is important or not.

There are so many great benefits that you are going to see when it is time to work with data analysis and using it for your own business. It can help you to learn more about your industry and the customers who are going to purchase your products. Those who are able to gather this information and learn how to use it in the proper manner with the help of data analysis will be able to help you to gain a leg up on your competition and see some amazing results in the process.

Chapter 6: The Steps of a Data Analysis

With some of the ideas of a data analysis defined above to show us why this is so important, it is time for us to take a look at some of the steps that are so important to this process. When we know a bit more about some of the steps of this data analysis, and what we are able to do with it, we are going to find why we should use this method of learning from Big Data and then ensuring that your business will be able to use this information in order to get further ahead of the competition.

For most businesses, there isn't going to be any problem with a lack of information. In fact, these businesses are going to suffer from having too much information to handle, and they are not certain what they are supposed to do with it. This over-amount of data is going to make it harder to come up with a clear decision based on the data, and that can be a problem as well. With so much data to go and sort through, we need to get something more from the data.

This means that we need to know that the data we have is right for the questions that we want to be answered. We need to know how we can draw some accurate conclusions from the data that we are working with. And we need data that is going to be able to take on and inform our decision-making process.

In all, we need to make sure that we have the best kind of data analysis set up and ready to go. With the right process and tools set up for our data analysis, something that may have seemed like too much in the beginning and like an overwhelming amount of stuff to go through will then become a simple process that is clear and easy as possible.

To help us get all of this done, we need to go through some of the basic steps that are needed to use this data to make better decisions overall. There are a lot of ways that we are able to divide this all up and make it work better for our needs, but we are going to divide this up into five steps that we are able to use and rely on to see some of the best results overall. Some of the steps that we can use to help make our data analysis more productive for better decision making in the company include:

Defining Your Question

The first step that we need to undertake when it comes to working on data analysis is to define the main question that we would like to handle. You should not just randomly work with the data that is on hand and hope that it shows you something. Because this is just going to get you lost and confused in the process. You need to have a clear picture of where you want to go and what you would like to learn from this data, and then work from there.

In your data analysis, you need to start out with the right questions. Questions are important, but we need to make sure that they are concise, measurable, and clear. Design the questions so that they are able to either qualify or disqualify some of the potential solutions that you are looking for on a specific problem or opportunity.

For example, you may want to start out with a problem that you are able to clearly define. Maybe you are a government contractor, and you find that your costs are rising quite a bit. Because of this, you are no longer able to submit a competitive contract for some of the work that you are doing. You will want to go through with this and figure out how to deal with the business problem. One of the questions that you may be taking a look at right now in order to help you solve this problem could be, "Can the company reduce its staff without compromising quality?"

Set up Clear Measurements

The next thing that we need to be able to do here is make sure that we are able to set up some clear priorities on your measurements. This is one that we will be able to break down into two subsets to help us out. The first part is that we need to decide what we want to measure. And then the second thing we need to decide is how to measure it.

So, let's start with the first part of deciding what we would like to measure. Going with the example of being a government contractor from before, we would have to take this time to consider what kind of data is needed in order to answer that question we posed in the beginning. In this case, you would first need to gather up information on the number and the cost that you have for that current staff and the amount of time that these employees are going to spend on business functions that are necessary.

When we are going through and answering this kind of question, there are going to be a number of other questions that we need to answer as well to help us figure out the options that we need to take as well. For example, we would want to see if there are any employees we could do without if the staff is under-utilized in their current jobs, and what you could do to help out with some of this.

And then, we are going to get to the decision that we want to measure. When doing this, we need to make sure that we are considering any of the objections, the reasonable ones, of stakeholders and others who are working with the company. They may be worried about what would happen if you reduced the staff, and then there was a big surge in demand shortly afterward, and you were not able to hire more people in the right amount of time.

Once we are done with that first step, it is time for us to make some decisions on how to measure. Thinking about how we are able to measure the data that we have is going to be just as important here, especially before we go through the phase of collecting data because the measuring process is going to either back up our analysis or discredits it later on. There are a lot of different questions that you are going to ask in this stage, but some of the most important ones to consider will include:

1. What is the time frame that we are looking at?
2. What is the unit of measure that we are relying on?
3. What factors are important to consider in all of this.

Collect the Data

After we have had some time to go through and define our big problem and then work on the measurements that we are going to use, it is time for us to move on to collecting the data. With the question defined and the measurement priorities set, it is now time for us to go through and collect the data. As we organize and collect the data, there are going to be a lot of important points that we must keep in mind with this will include:

1. Before you go out and collect some new data, you need to determine what information that we need to work with. We can look through some of the existing databases and some of the existing sources that we have on hand. You need to go through and collect some of this data first because it is simple and easier and can save a lot of money as well. We can move out to some other sources later, as well, if we need more information.

2. During this process, we also need to determine what naming system and file storing system we would like to use. This is going to make it easier for your team members to collaborate with one another. This process is going to save some time and will prevent members of your team from wasting time and money by collecting the same kind of information more than once.

3. If you would like to gather up data through interviews and observations, then you need to go through and develop an interview template ahead of time. This is going to ensure that we are able to save some time and that there is some continuity that goes on in this process as well.

4. And finally, we need to be able to keep the collected data that we have as organized as possible. We can work with a log that has the collection dates and add in the notes about sources as you would like. This should also include some data normalization that you may have performed as well. This is going to be important because it will validate the conclusions that you make down the road.

As you go through this process, we need to make sure that we are taking care of some of the data that we are working with. This means that we need to get it all organized, the values handled, and the duplicates took care of before you try to do some of the analysis that we want to do.

Since you are getting the data from a lot of different sources, and you are going to work with data that may be incomplete and not perfect along the way, we need to be careful here. It is hard to know whether the data is going to be perfect or that you are able to use it the way that you want. And if the information is in the wrong format, or it is not taken care of and the missing values and more are taken care of, then it is going to be hard to go through and get the algorithm to work.

The first thing that we need to do with this is to make sure that the data is in the same format. Usually, the best way to handle this is for us to go through and put all of the information in a standardized database that we can look at. We can use this in our storage service and make sure that all of the data we bring is in just put through that database and ready to go.

From there, we are tenable to focus on dealing with some of the errors that are found in that data. We want to make sure that the outliers, the missing values, and the duplicates are gone. For the most part, the outliers are things that you are going to need to ignore and get rid of. If there are a number of these, and they all end up in the same spot in the process, then you should take a look at this to see what is going on and if this is new information that you should pay attention to. But for most of these, you will find that they are not worth your time and should just be ignored.

From there, we are going to look at the missing values. When you get information from the real world, there are going to be times when there is a missing value in one of the parts that you are working with. You can choose to either delete these if there are just a few, or you can go through and replace these missing values with the mean of the other values that are in this column or row. It is up to you what you would like to do with these missing values to ensure that your information is as accurate as possible.

And finally, we need to deal with some of the duplicate values that are present in the set of data. If there are a lot of duplicate values that show up in some of the data, then we are going to find that this will skew a lot of the numbers that we have and the results that we will get. This is why we need to take care of them, so we can really see the true values that are inside of it.

You can go through here and figure out how much of the duplicate you would like to keep, and how much you would like to get rid of during your time. It is best to usually limit it as much as possible. Sometimes, this is keeping duplicates down to just two, and sometimes, it means only making sure that all of the entries are only in there once. It is up to us to figure out which method to go with.

Analyze the Data

After you have been able to collect the data, which is something that is going to take some time, we will then need to go through and start analyzing the data. We are going to start out with this by manipulating the data, and there are a number of methods that we are able to use to make this happen. For example, we may decide to plot that information out and then find out what correlations are there or do a pivot table in Excel.

The pivot table is going to be useful in order to help us sort out and filter the data by different variables and then make it easier for us to calculate out what the minimum, maximum, mean, and even the standard deviation of the data that we are working with. This can give us a lot of great information that makes it easier for us to get going and to get a better understanding out of the data we have.

As we work on the process of manipulating the data that we have, you may find that you already have the exact data that we need. But, of course, life doesn't always work out as nicely as we would like, and you need to either go out and collect some more data to work with or revise the original question that we are working with. Either way, you will find that this initial analysis of trends, variations, outliers, and correlations will help us to focus the data analysis that we do in order to better answer our questions and any of the objections that others may have in the process as well.

During this step, we will find that software and tools that work well with data analysis are going to be really helpful through all of this. There are a lot of good packages that work for helping us to get through all of this and will ensure that we are able to get some of the work done that we want with statistical data analysis. However, in many cases, you will be just fine with using something as simple as Microsoft Excel when it is time to find a tool for decision making. You need to go through all of this stuff.

Interpret the Results

After we have gone through the process of analyzing our data, which is going to take some time to accomplish and will often require some training and testing of your data through the algorithm to make sure that it works the way that you want, it is time for us to go through and interpret the results that we have. as we are going through this process and interpreting the analysis that we have, keep in mind that you are never going to be able to completely prove your hypothesis true 100 percent. But you can go through and reject the hypothesis. This means that no matter how much of this data you are able to collect, it is still possible for it to interfere with the results that we have.

As we are going through the process of interpreting our results, there are a few questions that we need to ask ourselves about this data as well. Some of these major questions are going to include:

1. Is the data able to answer the original question that we had in the beginning and how?
2. Does the data help us to defend against the objects that were raised and how?
3. Are there any limitations to the conclusion that we have, or any angles that you have not considered?

If the interpretation that you have about the data is able to hold up under these questions and considerations, then it is likely that you are working with a conclusion that is productive. The only remaining step here is to use the results of your data analysis to help decide which course of action is the best one for you to work with.

By following the steps that are outlined in this chapter for your data analysis, you will find that it will help you to make some better decisions for your business. The main reason for this is that your choices are going to be backed up by data that has been collected in a robust manner and analyzed as well. With practice, it is possible for your data analysis to provide us with faster and more accurate results. This means, in the long run, that you are going to be able to make better and more informed decisions that help your company to run more efficiently than before.

Chapter 7: The Importance of Big Data

A big part of what we are going to see with our data analysis is the use of big data. Big data, to make it simple, is going to be large and really complex sets of data, especially the ones that come from new sources of data. These are going to be so voluminous in most cases that traditional software to process this data isn't going to be able to manage it very well. But the issue isn't how much data there is or how much data you are able to collect. It is more about what you are able to learn from that data instead. When a company uses them in the proper manner, they will be able to find out the best solutions to address business problems that may have been hard to tackle before.

One of the first things that we need to take a look at when we are working with the idea of big data is the three Vs. The first one is going to be volume. The amount of data that you are working with here is going to matter. With big data, you are going to need to process high volumes of unstructured and low-density data. This can be data that has an unknown value, such as the data feeds from Twitter, clickstreams on a mobile app or webpage, or even equipment that is enabled with some sensors.

For some companies, the data isn't going to be as complicated as all that we listed above. Instead, they could just be dealing with tens of terabytes of data. For others, it could be even more. No matter what it is, big data is going to include a lot of different types of data that the business is going to use in the hopes of really gathering a lot of information to put them ahead of the competition.

The second V that we need to focus on is going to be the velocity. This is going to be the fast rate at which data is received and sometimes acted on. In most cases, the highest velocity of data streams right into the memory rather than it being written onto a disk. Some of the internet-enabled smart products that customers like to use are going to operate on an idea of real-time, or at least near real-time, and they are going to require from us some action and real-time evaluation in order to be as successful as possible.

And finally, we need to look at the variety. This is going to refer to the many different types of data that are available for us to use. Traditional types of data that we used in the past were seen as structured and this allowed them to easily fit into a database that was relational. This also made it a lot easier to sort through the information and find the insights and predictions with some of the tools that we had in the past.

But with the rise of big data, we find that some of the structured data is not as prevalent, and we are relying more on types of data that are unstructured. Semi-structured and unstructured types of data, including video, audio, and text, are going to require some additional preprocessing before we are able to use them because this is necessary to derive meaning and support the metadata overall as well.

This is just the start of what we are able to see with the big data, though. Over the years, we are able to find that there are two more Vs that we are able to add to this process as well. And these are going to include the value and the veracity of the data that we are working with as well.

To start with, data is going to have some sort of intrinsic value. But it is not going to be very useful to our business until we are able to discover that value. Something that is equally as important is how truthful the data is, and how much we are able to rely on it in the first place. In a world were data has become capital, it is important to make sure that the data you have is the most important.

Think about some of the biggest tech companies throughout the world. And you will quickly realize that a large part of the value that they are able to offer to their customers is going to come from the data they have. This is the same data that they are analyzing all of the time in order to develop some new products and produce their things in a more efficient manner.

Some of the breakthroughs that have happened recently have helped to really reduce the amount that it costs to store data and compute it. This is going to make it so much easier and less expensive to store this data than ever before. And with an increased volume of big data less expensive and more accessible, you are able to gather up what you need to make precise and accurate decisions for your business.

Finding value in big data isn't going to be just about analyzing it, though this is a big benefit that a lot of companies are going to work with. It is going to be an entire process of discovery, one that requires analysts who are insightful, business users, and executives who are able and willing to ask the right questions, recognize the patterns that are there, make assumptions that are informed, and predict behavior overall.

Although the idea of big data is relatively new, the originals of sets of data that were really large can go back to the '60s or earlier, when the world of data was just starting out. This was also the time when the first data centers showed up and the development of a tool that many businesses know a lot about, the relational database.

It was then around 2005 that people began to realize just how much data was generated by users of online services like YouTube and Facebook. Hadoop, which is an open-sourced framework that was designed to help us store and then analyze sets of big data, was then developed that same year to handle all of this interest in the data as well. It is also true that the NoSQL platform gained some popularity during this time as well.

The development of these kinds of frameworks, and there are more now since there is also a rise in interest in this topic, was essential to helping big data grow. This is simply due to the fact that they were there to make big data a whole lot easier for the analyst to work with, and definitely cheaper to store that data. In the years since that time, the volume of big data has really skyrocketed. Users are still able to generate a large amount of data, but it is not really just humans who are doing all of this any longer.

Thanks to the beginning of the Internet of Things, or IoT more devices and objects are going to be connected to the internet. This means that we are able to gather information on the usage patterns of the customer and even see how well a product is doing at the time. Thanks to the start of machine learning, which we will talk about in the next chapter, we have found that we are getting more software and tools that can help us to deal with all of this data.

While the world of big data has come a long way since it first began, we know that the usefulness of all this data is not going to fade anytime soon. Cloud computing has expanded the possibilities of big data even more because they offer a truly elastic kind of scalability, where developers are able to simply spin up some ad hoc clusters and then test a subset of that data in the manner that we need.

There are a number of benefits that we will be able to see when we are working with big data. Some of these benefits are going to include:

1. Big data will make it possible for us to gain answers that are more complete to some of our major business problems. The reason that we can come up with more complete answers is that we now have more information at our disposal than before

2. More complete answers thanks to the information that we have been able to gather means that we are going to have more confidence in the data that we are collecting. This is going to provide us with a brand new way to tackle some of the problems that come to us in business.

However, while there are a lot of promises and potential that comes with big data, we have to take a look at some of the challenges that can show up as well. First, big data is going to include a ton of data. Although there are new technologies that have been developed to handle data storage, the volumes of data are doubling in size every two years. This makes it hard for companies to keep pace with this data and to find ways to store and use it in the most effective manner possible.

Big data is going to provide us with some new insights that can really open up some new opportunities and business models. But to get started with this, there are three key actions that we need to talk about first. To start with this, we need to work on integration. Big data is going to bring together a lot of data from disparate sources and various applications. The traditional mechanisms of data integration are generally not expandable to some of the work that we see. This kind of data is going to require us to work with new strategies and technologies in order to analyze the big sets of data at a terabyte or sometimes even a petabyte scale.

During the process of integration, we are going to bring in the data, process it, and then make sure that it is formatted and available in the right form. Once all of this has happened, your business analysts can then go through the writing process to work with the data and start putting it through the algorithms that are needed for success.

Then we need to move on to the managing step. Big data is going to require a lot of storage from us. Your storage solution is going to vary based on how you would like to handle the data. It can be on the premises of the business, on the cloud, and sometimes, it is a combination of both. You can then store the data in any kind of form you would like, and then bring about the desired requirements for processing and the necessary process engines to those sets of data when they are needed.

Many times, a business is going to choose the solution for storage that they want to use according to where the data is residing right now. The cloud is gaining a lot of popularity because it is going to support your current computing requirements, and then it will enable you to spin up some of the resources that you need in the process.

And finally, we are going to work with the process of analyzing. Your investment with big data is going to be able to pay off big when we are analyzing and acting on your data. Get some new clarity with the visual analysis that you are using out of that set of data. And you can take your time to explore the data a bit more to make some new discoveries.

This is also the time of the process where you are going to share some of your findings with others. You can build up models of data with machine learning and artificial intelligence and then put this data to work for your needs. Make sure that you are keeping those biases out of the process to get the most accurate results possible.

There is so much data that is out in the world, and many companies have found that there is a good deal of value that they are able to see with all of this data based on where they gather it from and what they choose to do with it. Learning what big data is all about and how your business is able to work with it can make a big difference in the amount of success that your business will be able to see overall.

Chapter 8: A Look at Machine Learning

One topic that almost goes hand in hand with what we are talking about in data analysis and data science is that of machine learning. This is an interesting topic that we are going to spend some of our time on now because of all the great features and more that we are able to do with it. To start, machine learning is going to be a discipline of artificial intelligence that is geared towards developing technology to handle things in a manner similar to how a human would, giving the machine or the system its own kind of intelligence.

Machine learning is a unique process because it is going to allow a computer to handle some new situations through experience, observation, self-training, and analysis as well. There are already so many situations where we are able to work with this machine learning in order to get some of the results that we are looking for, and when it comes to analyzing the data that we have, you will find that machine learning is one of the best ways to do this.

Machine learning is going to be able to facilitate the continuous advancement of computing through exposures to new scenarios, help with testing, and lots of adaptations of the computer. And all of this is done while the computer employs pattern and trend detection for improved decisions in the future, although not identical, situations, later on.

There are a lot of terms that go together when we are talking about data science and working on our own data analysis, and being able to keep them separate and knowing how all of these will work is important. For example, it is not uncommon for machine learning to get confused with the process of knowledge discovery in databases, or KDD, or data mining. All of these are going to share a similar kind of methodology to get things done, but they will be used in different manners and are important in different manners.

There are a lot of different methods of working with machine learning, and figuring out how these work together and differently is going to be so important to learn what we are able to do with it in the present and in the future someday.

There is already so much that we are able to do when we talk about machine learning that it is no wonder that so many people are interested in learning what this machine learning is all about, and how they can use it for some of their own business needs. We see this kind of learning in situations like search engines, voice recognition devices that we use as personal assistants, our phones, recommendation sites on many sites, and even some of the marketing that we see when shopping online.

And this is just the beginning of what we will be able to do with the help of machine learning. We will find that as this technology starts to evolve a bit more in the future, we are going to find a lot more examples of how this can work. But when it comes to working with data analysis, machine learning is one of the best things around.

This is because we can use some of the algorithms that are a part of machine learning to help us to sort through the data and learn from it. We just spent some time talking about big data and how much data is out there for us to sort through. Imagine how bad it would be to handle this on your own and manually. This is going to be a process that is too difficult to handle and would take too long. But with the algorithms that are ready through machine learning, you will be able to sort through your data and see the great predictions and insights that we want.

Now that we have that little introduction, it is time to get into some more details about what this machine learning process is all about. This is basically a new type of programming, or newer compared to some of the other programming options that we have seen in the past, that will focus on helping the computer learn and get smarter, without the programmer having to go in and figure out all of the results and all of the answers ahead of time. This allows the program or the technology to do a lot of things that it wouldn't have been able to do in the past.

With machine learning, you are teaching the computer or the program to use its own experiences with the user in the past in order to perform better in the future. An example of this would be a program that can help with spam email filtering. There are a few methods that can work in this instance, but the easiest one would be to teach the computer how to categorize, memorize, and then identify all the emails in your inbox that you label as spam when they enter your email. Then, if some new emails come in later that match what is already on your email list, the program would be able to mark these as spam without any work on your part.

While this kind of memorization method is the easiest technique to program and work with, there are still some things that will be lacking with it. First of all, you are missing out on the inductive reasoning in the program, which needs to be there for efficient learning. As a programmer, it is much better to go through and program the computer so that it can learn how to discern the message types that come in and that are spam, rather than trying to get the program to memorize the information.

Let's see if we are able to make sure this process stays as easy to work with as possible without adding in any confusion to the process. Maybe you are working with a program that will allow your computer to do a scan of any emails that are considered spans that are in this folder on your computer. From this scan, the program is able to take a look at a new email that comes into your account and figure out whether it is considered spam or not based on the words and phrases that are found inside of it. Then the algorithm would place some emails in the spam in that folder, and let the others come through.

This is a great method to use to help out with sorting your emails and everything that comes with them, but we still need to use a bit of caution with this one, especially in the beginning. When the algorithms are doing the work that it should, the computer can still get things wrong on occasion. It needs to be able to learn along the way, and figure out the right way to behave for you before you are able to use it on a regular basis.

Benefits of Working with Machine Learning

Now that we know a bit more about the work of machine learning and what we are able to do with it, it is time to take a look at some of the benefits that come with machine learning, and how we are able to work with this to get the results that we would like. There are a number of benefits that come with machine learning and making sure that we realize how these work and how we are able to make them work for our own needs can be important as well.

The first benefit is that machine learning can make our systems work in a similar manner as a human can on certain problems. We will see though that these models are going to be more efficient than what we will be able to see with a person. Machine learning and the algorithms that come with it are going.

Machine learning can also help us to sort through a lot of data in a short amount of time. Manually going through all of the data that you have with a data analysis may seem like a great idea, but take one look at all of the data that you have been able to collect, and you will quickly become overwhelmed and worried about how it will ever get done. With some of the traditional methods of business intelligence, this is not something that is easily done.

But when we add in some of the data analysis that we want to accomplish, we will find that we are going to be able to work with machine learning in order to see some of the best results. There are many algorithms that we are able to work with in order to sort through the data. And as long as you have trained and tested the data in the proper manner, you will see that these can give us accurate results in no time.

There are many different algorithms that we are able to use with machine learning. As you do more work with the idea of machine learning, you will find that there are a ton of algorithms and more that you are able to work with. This is good news because you will find that the data you have is very diverse, and some of the ways that you would like to handle the data will be complicated as well. This is never a one-size-fits-all kind of process in data analysis, and machine learning is able to fit the bill pretty well for you.

You will find that with the help of machine learning, you will be able to choose and train out the algorithm that is going to be the best for your needs. And if you do different projects over time, you can definitely find the algorithms that are going to be the best for you. There are always a lot of options that come with machine learning and all of the algorithms that are there with them and being able to make these work, and picking out the right one, will be able to help you to see the best results.

We will find that machine learning is able to take on a lot of the complicated tasks that we would like, the ones that are often hard to handle with other forms of business tools and business intelligence. One of the ways that we are able to use the idea of machine learning is that it is able to help us with some of the tasks of programming that are more complicated and hard. There are going to be some tasks in your programming where traditional programming is not going to work that well, and you will be able to bring in machine learning in order to get a good handle on all of it as well.

There is just so much that we are able to do when it comes to machine learning, and it is definitely something that businesses are able to use on a regular basis to see some great results as well. There are already a lot of different things that we are able to do when it comes to working with machine learning overall. We can see this in spam filters, in voice and facial recognition, and so much more.

And as time goes on in the future, you will find that there is a lot of potentials that you are going to be able to see this technology for. It is going to be a really unique thing that we are able to work with over time, and when you are able to really adjust it for the needs that you have for data analysis or another process, you will find that machine learning can be really adaptable and will be able to handle many of the problems and issues that we have in the future.

As we can see, there are a lot of benefits that come with machine learning, but there are going to be a few challenges that come with this kind of process as well. For example, depending on the kind of algorithm you would like to work with, the computation costs can be high. This is going to make it inefficient or too expensive for the things that you would like to accomplish and can make it a bad choice to work with overall as well.

In addition, depending on how much data you are working with and what task you would like to accomplish, you may find that there is an easier process to work with, one that is able to handle some of the work that is needed with machine learning in a more efficient manner and still get you the results that you want. You have to determine whether machine learning is actually the right choice for your needs or not before getting things that started.

Supervised Machine Learning

Now that we have had some time to take a look at machine learning and all that it has to offer, it is time for us to dive in a bit about the three types of machine learning that are going to be important to the work that we are doing. The three types of machine learning that are going to be important to the work that we will do in this guidebook will include supervised, unsupervised, and reinforcement machine learning.

When it is time to work with machine learning, the first type of algorithm that you are able to work with is going to be supervised machine learning. This one is going to be the type that will include a human who is using the system, and then this person will need to provide the computer with the right input and the corresponding output that needs to go with it. At the same time, the programmer is going to need to be the one that provides some feedback to the system based on how accurate the predictions are from that algorithm at the time. The feedback that is provided is going to be determined based on how accurate the system is with their predictions.

What this is supposed to mean for us is that the trainer, or the programmer, needs to be able to show the system a bunch of examples, and then the trainers have to show the system what is right and what is not. Then, as the system learns from what the trainer is telling it, it will be able to get smarter and work on improving itself even when the trainer is no longer there to provide it with the feedback it needs.

After the trainer has spent some time training the computer and helping this algorithm work, the algorithm will be able to apply the information that it has learned from the data earlier on so it can take a new input and make the best predictions possible. The concept that we are going to see with supervised learning is going to be similar to what we are going to see when a teacher is trying to show their class something new.

For this, the teacher is going to provide some kind of lesson to the students and then provide some examples to help drive the point home. The students will take a look at the examples and can gain some new knowledge and some new rules from the examples that their teacher gives. They are then able to take that knowledge that they gain in the process and apply it to a lot of different situations, even when the new situations don't really match up, but are similar to the examples that they were able to get in the classroom from the teacher.

When we take a look at this supervised machine learning, it is going to be important that we know the differences between the classification problems and the regression problems that we are going to handle. The regression problem is going to happen when the target is a numeric value that we need to work with. But the classification kinds of problems are going to include a tag or a class. The regression tag is going to be important because we can use it in situations where we are trying to figure out the average costs of all the properties in the town, while the classification problem will be used in order to figure out what flower type is in a picture by looking at the color and the size of the flower petals..

We have to remember that at times, the accuracy that comes with this one is going to suffer a bit when you have unlikely, impossible, and incomplete values that are being used with your training data. Being able to take a look at some of the training data that you want to work with, before placing it through the algorithm, and getting a better understanding of how this will work can really provide us with a big difference in how the data is going to work, and how accurate it can be.

Now, we need to first take a look at some of the positives and benefits that are going to come to us when we work with the supervised machine learning form. There are a lot of good qualities to working with these algorithms, which is why we are talking about them now and why we are looking at them as a part of our work. Some of the different benefits and advantages that you are going to see when it is time to work with supervised machine learning algorithms will include:

1. This kind of learning is going to allow you to collect data, or produce an output of data from experience that is had in the past.
2. This kind of learning is going to help you to optimize some of the performance criteria with the help of your experience.
3. This kind of learning is going to be useful when it is time to solve a lot of the different real-world problems of computation that can show up.

With this said, there are also a few disadvantages that can come up when using supervised learning methods. This is why there are other forms of learning in machine learning, including unsupervised and reinforcement learning. Some of the disadvantages that you may encounter when working with supervised learning include:

1. It is possible for the boundary of decisions to be overtrained. This happens when the training set doesn't have any examples of what you want inside a class.
2. You have to take the time to select a ton of good examples from each class as you go through the training process. Without these examples, the classifier is not going to know how you would like it to behave.
3. Classifying out some of the big data that you have can turn into a big challenge.

As we can already see when we work on this kind of machine learning, there are a lot of things that we will be able to do with it, and a lot of projects where we are able to pull this out and get the best results. It is not the only kind of algorithm that you are able to use within machine learning, but it is one of the best ones that you can focus on.

Unsupervised Machine Learning

Now that we know a little bit more about the basics and the benefits of supervised machine learning, it is time to move on to the second type of machine learning that is important to some of the work that we want to work with. While there are a lot of benefits that come with using supervised machine learning algorithms, there are going to be a few challenges as well. And these challenges are the exact reason why we need to work with something like unsupervised machine learning. With these kinds of algorithms, we do not need to have a programmer present, and we don't need to provide feedback to the system at all. The system, when you add in the right algorithm with it, will be able to handle all of this on its own.

This is part of the neat things that you are able to do when it comes to machine learning. You will find that this algorithm will help your system to figure out the outputs on its one and can provide the user based on whatever input, which is something that is unknown ahead of time. That the person is going to use there, any approach that is known is going to be considered the iterative approach or deep learning, is going to be the thing that we use to help review our data before we arrive at the conclusions that we need from this data.

The way that this is going to work is that it allows this kind of algorithm a way to handle a lot of the different processing tasks that you would like to work with, and many of the tasks that fall into this are going to be more complex with some of the things that we are going to not be able to do with supervised machine learning.

A good example of how this can work is with those recommender systems that you may find when you are shopping online. These have to use unsupervised machine learning algorithms in order to figure out what is going to be the item that you are the most likely to purchase next based on the answers that you have given before.

This particular unsupervised machine learning algorithm is going to derive what it should suggest that you purchase next based on the items you have glanced through before, and then once that you have actually purchased. The algorithm then is going to estimate the customers that you are going to resemble the most based on your purchases and their purchases and can take all of this information to provide a good recommendation on what you should purchase at that store next.

As we mentioned a little bit before, there is more than one type of machine learning that you can work with. Supervised learning is the first one. It is designed for you to show examples to the computer and then you teach it how to respond based on the examples that you showed. There are a lot of programs where this kind of technique is going to work well, but the idea of showing thousands of examples to your computer can seem tedious. Plus, there are many programs where this is not going t work all that well.

This is a good example of how the idea of unsupervised machine learning algorithms is going to come into play with us. This algorithm is able to help us learn from some of our mistakes or examples without someone being there, providing them with some of the feedback or the responses that are needed. These algorithms are all on their own to figure out the best way to behave, all on its own.

There are going to be many different options that you are able to work with when it is time to handle these algorithms, and when you use this king of algorithm you are able to open up a ton of doors to different challenges and processes that we are able to do. This is an exciting part of machine learning that we need to explore more as time goes on because it allows our computers to do a lot of things that we did not think possible in the past.

Now, when compared to working with supervised machine learning, you will find that there are a lot of new challenges that you are able to handle when you work with unsupervised learning. But even though they are different, it is time for us to take a look at some of the reasons why we would want to work with this kind of learning algorithm. Some of these include:

1. This kind of learning is helpful for finding all kinds of patterns that are unknown in your data.
2. This kind of learning is going to help you find out the different features that you can use for categorization.

3. This kind of learning is going to happen in real-time so that all of the input data to be labeled and analyzed in the presence of learners happens.
4. You will find that it is often easier for us to get ahold of data that is unlabeled from our computer compared to getting labeled data, and unsupervised learning helps with this.

There are a lot of different ways that we are able to apply the use of unsupervised learning. First, clustering is going to be one of the methods that are useful here, and it automatically splits up the data set that we have available into groups. The data will be placed into a group based on the similarities that it has to the other data points in that group. In addition, the detection of anomalies can discover a lot of the unusual points of data that are in your set. It is going to be useful for many scenarios, including finding any transactions that are fraudulent.

You will find that working with unsupervised machine learning is going to be one of the best ways for us to work with some of the work that we want to see with data analysis. These algorithms are able to handle a lot of the different parts that we need to work with for writing our algorithms and sorting through some of the different types of data that we want to work with. Make sure to take some time to look at some of the different algorithms that we are able to use with unsupervised machine learning.

Reinforcement Machine Learning

The third type of machine learning that we are able to take a look at is going to be known as reinforcement machine learning. This one is a little bit different than what we are going to see with some of the options along the way, even though it is going to share some similarities to what we are going to see with the unsupervised machine learning that we talked about before.

However, we will find that reinforcement learning is going to work on programming the system with feedback that is negative and positive based on what solution the machine is going to provide to us. Since this one is based on a true and false idea, and the system is going to be able to work with this to see the best results.

With this kind of algorithm, you will find that some errors are just fine within the learning process. This is because the errors are going to help the system to learn a little bit better. They are going to be associated back with some kind of penalty that you put in, which can be something like a loss of cost, loss of pain, and lost in time. When we work with reinforced machine learning, you will find that there are going to be some actions that can succeed more, and then there are some actions that are not able to succeed all that well, and this is how this kind of algorithm is going to be able to learn along the way.

Machine learning processes are often going to be similar to what we would view with data mining and predictive modeling. In both of these cases, the patterns are important because they can be adjusted inside of the program in the manner that you need. A good example that we can use machine learning is the recommender system from above, but it often focuses more on unsupervised machine learning rather than reinforcement learning. But there are some times when the reinforcement machine learning is going to be a better choice to work with.

There are some people who see reinforcement learning as the same thing as unsupervised learning because they are so similar, but it is important to understand that they are different. First, the input that is given to these algorithms will need to have some mechanisms for feedback. You can set these up to be either negative or positive based on the algorithm that you decide to write out.

So, whenever you decide to work with reinforcement machine learning, you are working with an option that is like trial and error. Think about when you are working with a younger child. When they do some action that you don't approve of, you will start by telling them to stop, or you may put them in time out or do some other action to let them know that what they did is not fine. But, if that same child does something that you see as good, you will praise them and give them a ton of positive reinforcement. Through these steps, the child is learning what is acceptable behavior and what isn't.

This can seem a bit complicated to work with as we go with this. To make sure that we can keep this as simple as possible, we need to take a closer look at how this kind of algorithm is going to work. Reinforcement learning is going to work on an algorithm that is based on trial and error, and it is going to be able to make decisions based on what it learns is right, and what it learns is wrong. It is a good algorithm to work with any time that we would like an algorithm that can handle these decisions, after going through its training and testing, without making mistakes, and ensuring that it still has a good outcome in the end.

Of course, we have to remember that this process and getting the algorithm to work properly is going to take some time for the program to learn what it needs to do. But you are able to add this to the code that you are trying to write out so that the program has the best chance to behave in a manner that we are hoping for.

Before we move on from this topic, though, we need to make sure that we fully understand some of the key points that come with this kind of reinforcement learning. There are a number of benefits to this process, and the main points that are going to help us to reach all of these benefits in an efficient manner will include:

1. Input. In reinforcement learning, the input needs to be an initial state from which the model is going to start.
2. Output: It is possible to have a lot of different outputs. The number of outputs will depend on how many solutions there are to any given problem that you are working with.
3. Training: The training is going to be based on the input that you provide. The model is going to need to return to a state and then the user is able to decide to either punish or reward the model based on the output that it provides.
4. The model is going to continue to learn over time. It doesn't just stop and never does any learning again.
5. The best solution is going to be based on which output is going to provide the highest reward.

We have already taken a look at how reinforcement learning is going to be similar to what we found with unsupervised machine learning, but let's look at some comparisons on how reinforcement learning is going to be similar and different from supervised learning.

As we can see, there are a lot of benefits that come with all of the different types of machine learning that you want to work with. It is often going to depend on what results you are trying to get and what data you would like to handle. Make sure to check out each of these to learn a little bit more about how these work and how you are able to use them for some of your own needs in data analysis.

Chapter 9: Your Course for the Pandas Library

Pandas

The next topic that we are going to spend some time taking a look at is the Pandas library. This is going to be one of the best libraries that we are able to work with in order to see some great results with data analysis. If you want to handle the process of data science, and you don't want to skip through and work with a lot of different parts as well, then the Pandas library is going to be one of the best ones for you to work with.

The Pandas library is going to stand for the Python Data Analysis Library, and it is going to be helpful with completing a lot of different things when it comes to data analysis and being able to do more of the mathematical work and more within the Python language as you would like. The Panda's name is going to be a derivative of the term panel data, which is going to be something that we see often in the field of data science to help out with multidimensional structured sets of data. No matter how the name started or what it is all going to mean to us, it is still a nice name to help us to complete some of our goals in this language.

You will find that when we are working with data analysis, there is a lot that Pandas can do to help change up the game of how we do our own coding throughout. In fact, this is going to be one of the more used and the most preferred tools out there when it is time to handle data munging and data wrangling in this language, and in other parts of this process as well. Pandas are going to be a free option to use as well and open source, which means that anyone is able to use it in order to handle their data in a safe, effective, and fast manner.

There are a lot of other libraries that are out there, but you will find that a lot of companies and individuals are going to love working with Pandas. One thing that is really cool about Pandas is that it is able to take data, whether it is from an SQL database, a TSV file or even a CSV file, and then it will take that information and create it into a Python object. This is going to be changed over to columns and rows and will be called a data frame, one that will look very similar to a table that we are going to see in other software that is statistical.

If you have worked with R in the past, then the objects are going to share a lot of similarities to R as well. And these objects are going to be easier to work with when you want to do work and you don't want to worry about dictionaries or lists for loops or list comprehension. Remember that we talked earlier about how loops can be nice in Python, but you will find that when it comes to data analysis, these loops can be clunky, take up a lot of space, and just take too long to handle. Working with this kind of coding language will help you to get things done without all of the mess along the way.

We talked a bit before about how you need to go through and do the steps that will get the Pandas library to install on your computer. It is best to install it at the same time that you are doing Python and the other libraries to make things easier and to ensure all of your libraries are ready to go. If you have not had time to do this yet, go ahead and do it now.

Once we have been able to go through and download the Pandas library, it is then time for us to get to work with all of the features and more that we are able to do with this library. There are going to be a ton of features in order to work with this library and spending some time learning more about it and how we are able to get it to work for us can really take us further with what we will be able to accomplish with this kind of library as well.

When you are ready and have had some time to mess around with some of the features that come with this library, then it is time for us to analyze some of the data that we have already gathered. There are usually three different methods that we will be able to bring out to work, as well. The three main methods that we are going to be able to use with this library will include:

1. You can convert a NumPy array, a Python list, or a Python dictionary over to the data frame that is available with Pandas.
2. You can open up a local file that is found on your computer with the help of Pandas. This is often going to be something like a CSV file, but it is possible that it could be something else like Excel or a delimited text file in some cases.
3. You can also choose to use this in order to open up a file, or another database that is remote, including a JSON or CSV that is located on a

website through a URL, or you can have the program read through it on a database or a table that is from SQL.

Now, you will find that there are going to be a few different kinds of commands that will go with all of these options that are above, so we are going to spend some time looking at them through this chapter. But there are a few commands to help us open up all of these files and more, no matter what they end up being in our code. The code that is necessary to make this happen for our needs and to ensure that we are able to open up our files with the help of Pandas is going to include the following:

pd.read_filetype()

Now, as we mentioned a bit before, there are going to be a variety of file types that work well with Python, and you can choose the ones that are going to be the best for your project. So, with the code above, you would want to replace the part of the code that says "filetype" with the actual type of file that you are using. You would need to give the name of the file, the path, or other options inside of the parenthesis. And inside of those parentheses, you can also pass any of the various arguments that you are going to relate to how to open your particular file.

You may find that while working on this that you will encounter a lot of arguments that you will then need to be able to choose from and to know all of these is going to take up a lot of time and commitment. To know all of them would be hard, and it is not always the most effective at all. There are many arguments, and since you will not likely use all of them for your needs, we are going to focus on just the few that are the most important to our needs, rather than trying to go through all of them and memorizing things we will not even need in the process.

With this kind of idea in mind, we need to spend some of our time trying to convert an object that are using over to Python, whether we are working with something like a dictionary or a list or another part of our program, ever so that it is going to work with the Pandas library as well. The basic command that we are going to use to make this happen includes:

pd.DataFrame()

For this one, the inside part of the parenthesis is where you are going to specify the different object or objects that you are creating the data frame from. This command is going to have a few different arguments that you are able to work with as well. In addition to doing the above, it is possible to go through and then save that particular data frame that you decide to work with on a lot of other types of files. This could include tables from SQL, JSON, Excel, and CSV. The general kind of code that you are going to be able to use to make this one work will include the following:

df.to_filetype(filename)

At this point, you have been able to load up the data, so now it is time for us to take a look and do a little bit of inspecting the data that we have available. We can start by taking a look at the data frame and seeing if it matches up with what we want. To do this, you can run the name of your chosen data frame to get the entire table, but you are also able to decide how much you get. For example, to get the first n amount of rows, you would use the function of df.heat(n) or if you would like to work with the last n number of rows, then you would need to do df.tail(n). The df.shape would be able to get you the number of rows and columns that you would like, and if you would like to get information on the memory, data type, and index, you would need to work with the df.info().

We can even take this a little bit further and work with the command of s.value_counts(dropna=False), and this one allows us to view the unique values and counts for the series, such as if you would work with one or a few columns. A useful command that we are going to need to spend some of our time here and is important to learn is the df.describe) function. This one is going to help us when it is time to input some of the summary statistics that come with the numerical columns. Also, remember that it is possible for a data scientist to go through and get the statistics on the whole series or data frame if needed.

This can all sound a little bit confusing at this point, but to ensure that we are getting the right part out of this and what it all means, we need to take a few moments to look at some of the commands that are available with Pandas that we are able to use. These are going to be helpful for ensuring that we can view and inspect any of the data that we are working on. Some of the commands that we need to work with here will include:

1. df.mean(): This function is going to help us get the mean of all our columns.
2. df.corr(): This function is going to return the correlation between all of the columns that we have in the frame of data.
3. Df.count(): This function is going to help us return the number of non-null values in each of the frames of data based on the columns.
4. Df.max(): The function is going to return the highest value in each of the columns.
5. Df.min(): This function is going to return the lowest value that is found in each of the columns that you have.
6. Df.median(): This is going to be the function that you can use when you want to look at each column and figure out the median.
7. Df.std(): This function is going to be the one that you would use in order to look at each of the columns and then find the standard deviation that comes with it.

When we get to this point, we then need to figure out some of the ways that we can use Pandas in order to help out with this selection of data that we have gathered up. One of the things that you will find that is easier to work with here is that Pandas can help you to select the data that you want, compared to having to select a value from the list or the dictionary.

As we go through this, you are able to select the column, or you can use this to help you complete a return column that has a label of a col as Series. And it is possible to go through and do a few columns so that you do end up with a return column as a brand new DataFrame. Another option to go with is to select by the position or even by an index, depending on what you would like to do with the data you have.

To make it easier to go through the data and then select that first row of the data set to get things done, you want to use the function of df.iloc[0, :] and to help you to pick out the first element of the first column that we want to bring out of that set of data, we would need to use the command of df.iloc[0 0]. You are able to work with the same code in different combinations so that when it is time to go through and select the index and the data that you want to work with, in particular, you can get it done.

With some of this done, and now that we have had some time to go through and select the type and amount of data that we would like to work with, there are still a few other tasks that we are able to do with the help of Pandas. There are a lot of options that we are able to work with here including grouping, sorting, and filtering to make sure that the data is put into the right place that we would like, and that we are then able to find it, without a struggle, to work on later.

As we can see here, there are a lot of different things that we are able to do when it is time to work with the Pandas library. The Pandas library is going to have a ton of features and abilities that can help us with every part of our data analysis along the way. And when we are working with the Python language along with the Pandas library, we will be able to handle all of our data analysis needs with as much ease as possible.

Chapter 10: The Importance of Matplotlib and Data Visualization

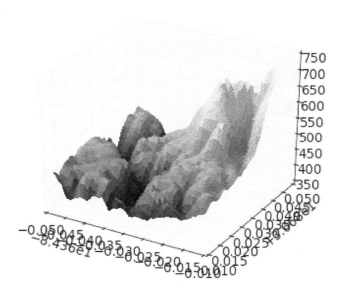

The final topic that we are going to take a look at in this guidebook is the importance of working with a data visualization when we are handling our work with data analysis. This is a great step to add to the process because it ensures that we are able to see the best results overall and will make it easier for us to actually see some of the complex relationships that are going to show up in the data. Missing out on this is going to make it harder for those who have to make decisions off your data analysis to learn what steps to take with their data and what predictions and decisions they should make.

In this chapter, we are going to take a look at a few different options when it is time to work with these data visuals. We are going to start out with some information on what the matplotlib is all about and how this is going to be able to help us to work with creating some of the different visuals you would like. And then, we will be able to move on and explore why these data visuals are so important to work with in the first place.

There are a lot of benefits that come with working on data visualization, and it is never a good idea for us to go through and assume that this is not important.

When you are ready to see how you can create some of your own data visuals and why they are so important to use in the first place, make sure to check out this chapter to help you get started.

What is Matplotlib?

There are a lot of different libraries that we are able to work with when it is time to handle visuals and other work of data analysis inside of our Python language. But the library that we are going to spend some time taking a look at in this chapter is one that is meant to work with the idea of data visualization and why this is so important to some of the work that we want to accomplish.

To start with, you will find that matplotlib is going to be a plotting library that is set up to work with Python. It is also going to be a numerical mathematics extension that works off the arrays that we see in NumPy. This means that if we want to work with the matplotlib library, we need to first make sure that we have NumPy, and sometimes other libraries as well, on our system and ready to go as well.

When we are working with Matplotlib, you will find that it is useful when it is time to provide an API that is object-oriented for embedding plots into applications that will work with some of the toolkits for GUI that is general-purpose. There is also going to be a procedural interface based on a state machine that will work similar to MATLAB, although these are both going to be completely different things from one another, and it is important to work with them in a different manner.

The matplotlib is a great library to work with, and it was originally written by John D. Hunter. It is also going to impress a lot of new programmers because it has a development community that is active. It is also going to be distributed with a license that is BSD so that it is easier for us to use the way that we would like overall.

There are a lot of really cool options that you are able to work with when it is time to handle the matplotlib library, and this opens up a lot of opportunities for you when it is time to pick out the different choices in visuals. There are many of these that you are able to work with, and thanks to the way that matplotlib is set up, you will be able to pick out almost any kind of visual that you would like to work with as well.

This means that if you want to make a chart, a pie graph, a bar graph, a histogram, or some other kind of chart, this library is going to have a lot of the additional parts that we are looking for when it is time to handle your data. Make sure to take a look at some of the different options that are provided with this library, and then pay attention to what we are able to do with them before picking the one that is the best for you.

There are also going to be a number of different toolkits that you are able to handle when it is time to work with Matplotlib. These toolkits are important because they are going to help us to really extend out the amount of functionality that we will see with this library. Depending on the one that you would like to work with, some of them are going to be separate kinds of downloads, and some are going to ship along with the source code that is found in this library, but their dependencies are going to be found outside of this library, so we have to pay attention to this as well. Some of the different toolkits that we are able to work with include:

1. The basemap: This is going to be a map plotting tool that we are able to use to help out with different types of projects of a map, coastlines, and political boundaries that we are going to see in here.

2. Cartopy: This is another good one to work with when it is time to handle maps and some of that kind of work. This is going to be a mapping library that will have object-oriented map project definitions and arbitrary point lines, image transformation, and even polygon capabilities as well.

3. This one can also come with a number of Excel tools if you would like to work with these as well. This makes it easier for us to use Excel as our database, and you will easily be able to set this up so that you are able to exchange data from your matplotlib library and Excel.

4. GTK tools that are going to allow us the ability to interface and work with the GTK+ library if you would like.

5. The Qt interface.

6. The ability to work with 3-D plots to help out with some of the visuals that you are going to want to use along the way.

7. Natgrid: This is going to be an interface that will allow us into the library of natgrid for gridding irregularly spaced data when you would like.

And these are just a few of the things that we will be able to do when it comes to using this library. There are a few other libraries that help with visuals if you would like, but we have to remember that this is one of the best ones to work with, and they will keep things as simple and easy to use as possible. And with all of the added and nice features that are going to come with this, you will be able to see some great results with your visuals as well.

What is Data Visualization, and Why is it Important?

One part that comes with the process of data analysis is working with data visualization. But often, this is one that companies are going to struggle with remembering because they don't think it is all that important for them to work with. They worry that this is going to be a waste of time and that they are just going to be able to work with the reports and spreadsheets along the way in order to get the best results.

But there are a lot of benefits that come with working with data visualization, and it is so important to not forget this part when you are working with data analysis. Data visualization makes it so much easier for us to go through and understand some of the complex data that is found, and learn what relationships are inside of that data when you need it the most.

Sure, you can go through all of the reports and the other documents that contain the results of your analysis and that comes from the algorithms that you use, but this does not make it easier to handle the data at all. Most people are going to be more visual in what they are doing, and they will be able to learn in a few minutes from some of the different visuals that they have, compared to spending several hours or more looking through the charts and diagrams that they have.

The good news is that these visuals are going to be simple to work with, and you will be able to create them with the help of the Matplotlib library that we talked about earlier. There are some other libraries that you are able to work with as well, but this is often one of the best because of all the features that are present in it and how many options you are able to use when it is time to create one of these data visuals.

There are also going to be a number of data visuals that you are able to work with as well. This is going to make it really easy for you to get started because you are able to choose the right visual that is the best for the data you have, and what you are trying to learn out of the data as well. For example, with the help of the matplotlib library and other options that are out there, you will be able to pick from options like a bar graph, pie graph histogram, and more.

Picking out the data visual that you would like to work with is going to take some time to handle, and it is something that you should handle with some good consideration as well. This is going to make it easier for us to make sure that the visual we pick is going to work with the data that we are choosing, and that we are really going to understand the complex relationships that we want to handle throughout this as well. Do not forget this step because it is going to be a very important part of the analysis and can make it a lot easier to handle some of the different things that we need to work on along the way.

Conclusion

Thank you for making it through to the end of *Python for Data Science*. Let's hope it was informative and able to provide you with all of the tools you need to achieve your goals, whatever they may be.

The next step is to get started with some of the work that we are able to do when it is time to work on both the Python language and data analysis as well. We are going to be able to realize a lot of different benefits when we are able to combine both of these together in order to get our business out and winning against our competition. This guidebook is going to take some time to not only learn some of the basics to some of the most advanced options that we can do with Python and its coding but also how to work with data analysis to help us learn about our competition and how to get ahead of the rest in our industry.

In this guidebook, we are going to take some time learning more about the Python language and what it all entails. We are going to spend our time looking at some of the basics, intermediate, advanced, and expert options of coding that you are able to do with this language as well. This is meant to help us get started with Python as a complete beginner, and then we are going to move on to become an expert when it is all said and done.

From there, it is time for us to move on to learn more about how we are able to take this language to the next level and really learn how to make this one work for some of our own needs. We are going to learn more about the process of data analysis, and how this is going to be able to help out the business to succeed. We then took some time to look at what the process of data analysis is all about, how to create our own data analysis and some of the steps that come with this process as well.

The end of this guidebook took a look at some of the other parts that we need to know in order to work with data analysis and more. We will explore some more about big data, we took a look at machine learning and the different parts that come with it, how to work with the Pandas library, and the importance of working with data visualization and the matplotlib library in order to help us finish up some of our work when we are completing a data analysis.

There are so many benefits that we are going to be able to get when it is time to work on data analysis for some of our own needs. There are also countless possibilities that you could do by using Python. The only limit that would hinder you is your imagination. Be creative with your code and how you construct them. When you are ready to get started with this data analysis and all that it entails with the help of your new skills in the Python coding language, make sure to check out this guidebook to help you get started.

Finally, if you found this book useful in any way, a review on Amazon is always appreciated!

www.ingramcontent.com/pod-product-compliance
Lightning Source LLC
Chambersburg PA
CBHW071131050326
40690CB00008B/1427